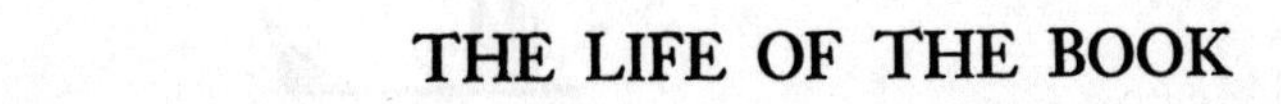

THE LIFE OF THE BOOK

HELLMU

THE LIFE OF

How the book is

written,

published,

printed,

sold, and

read

LEHMANN-HAUPT

THE BOOK

with line drawings by Fritz Kredel
and additional illustrations

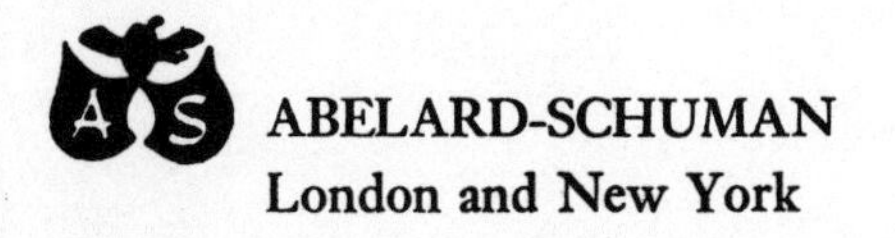
ABELARD-SCHUMAN
London and New York

Library of Congress Catalog Card Number — 57:5138

Designed by George T. Resch

Published by Abelard-Schuman Limited
London and New York

Published simultaneously in Canada by
Nelson, Foster & Scott Ltd.

Manufactured in the United States of America

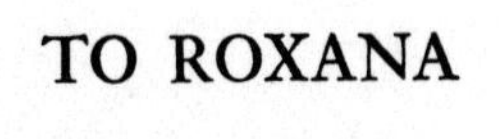

TO ROXANA

CONTENTS

ILLUSTRATIONS

Introduction

I once asked a boy named Thomas what he was going to be when he grew up. "Be Thomas," he said. This was a wonderful answer to what was perhaps a rather silly question.

I remember, when I was a teenager, how the question of what I was going to be worried me a good deal. But one day, when I was almost old enough to go to college, I met an old Scottish godmother of mine whom I had not seen for many years. She asked me what I was going to be. While I was searching for the proper words for an answer, she looked at me with bright and friendly eyes. "You know," she said, "a very good thing is to know something about everything and everything about something."

This was the magic formula that has guided me through the years. When my godmother bestowed her gift upon me, I already knew what this "something," about which I was going to try to know everything, was: it was *The Book*.

To become a publisher was my earliest ambition but, curiously enough, this is about the only profession connected with books that I have never had a chance to explore. I have worked at almost everything else in the book field at some time or other during the last thirty odd years: selling books old and new, some just off the press, others hundreds of years old; editing manuscripts to get them ready for the printer; designing books; proofreading; typesetting; reviewing books; exhibiting them; teaching the history of printing and books and how to design them; and writing books like this one.

I thought you might like to know this, in case you were wondering why this book that you now hold in your hands seems to take in so many different things, why it tries to tell you "everything about something."

Part I

HOW BOOKS ARE WRITTEN AND PUBLISHED

Chapter 1

WHAT IS A BOOK?

This question is not so easy to answer as one might think. We use the word "book" today to describe a great many different things. What we mean by "book" depends upon whether we are thinking about its form and appearance (what we call format), and the material out of which it is made, or about the purpose it is supposed to serve.

If we are considering physical format, we can call any object a book which is a gathering of a number of leaves held together along one of the four edges and protected at front and back with a cover of more or less durable material. In this very loose sense, not only a bible, a textbook, or novel, but also a magazine, a comic book, a notebook, a ledger, and even a checkbook can be called a "book."

If we are considering purpose, we can define the book as a means of visual communication. It tells a message through a series of what we call "graphic symbols" (written or printed words and pictures). It is distinguished in important ways from other forms of written or printed communications, such as letters and documents, newspapers, and periodicals. All these are usually shorter than books and as a rule they are not intended to last as long. A book, by contrast, is usually a fairly long, continuous body of communication; it often consists of several units carefully organized into parts, or chapters, and it sometimes consists of more than one volume. Also, and this is a very important point, books are the most suitable means for the permanent preservation of written material of lasting value.

In recent years another method has been developed for the same purpose: the microfilm. By photographing the pages of a book, or any other written or printed material, on a continuous roll of film, a large amount of information can be condensed into a small space. However, a special machine is necessary for reading a microfilm.

Of course, not all books can be considered valuable material of lasting importance. Many millions of inexpensive volumes are printed each year which are intended for easygoing, quick entertainment; they are read once and then discarded or passed along to someone else, like an old magazine.

But the most valuable service of the book lies in its permanency, in its capacity to preserve carefully selected observations, experiences, and artistic expressions of lasting value. Here is the important difference between books on the one hand and a great many other kinds of written and printed communications on the other.

It is to this kind of book that the following pages are devoted. You will find here the story of how such a book comes into being, how it is born as an idea in the head of an author, how it finds its way to a publisher, and how a single, typewritten manuscript is turned into an edition of many thousand identical copies. You will find out about the marvelous machines which make this possible, and discover how these machines are the result of many centuries of patient experimentation. You will read the wonderful story of the development of the art of bookmaking from the scrolls of the ancient peoples, and from the manuscripts in the medieval monasteries to Gutenberg's invention of printing with movable type, and you will learn about the astounding progress that has been made in the art of typography, of illustration, and of bookbinding since those early days.

You will also find out how a publisher today sells a new book, how it comes into the hands of the reader and reaches the shelves of libraries. You will read about the joys of book collecting and the wonderful things our libraries are doing for the people of this country. You will learn about the place of books in the modern world and their unique role in the years ahead.

Chapter 2

THE AUTHOR

How are books born? Well, most books start as an idea in the head of a man or a woman who wants to write a book.

When the writer starts to write, he knows or believes that what he has to say is important for other people. He feels that he has something new to say that has never been expressed before, or has not been said clearly or strongly enough or not so beautifully. He may feel that he has a better explanation than someone else for something we are trying to understand. He may have a good story to tell which he knows will entertain his readers.

There is one interesting thing about this: It often does not take an author long to get such an idea; sometimes it strikes him like a flash. Many of the great ideas which have had a deep influence on the course of human destiny have been very simple ones. They may have appeared like a sudden vision before the mind's eye of the author. But to turn such a dream into reality, to express it in words which can be read and understood by other people is often a long and tedious task. Some writers, like some painters or architects, spend a lifetime in trying to express ever more forcefully and convincingly what they feel they have to say. Dante, the great medieval Italian poet, for instance, started to write his *Divine Comedy* at the age of thirty-five, and he worked on it more or less for twenty years, until the time of his death in 1321.

John Milton, one of England's greatest poets, prob-

The author at work

ably spent something like fifteen or sixteen years in writing *Paradise Lost*. When it was first published, on August 20, 1667, Milton had actually been thinking about the subject for at least twenty-five years.

When the distinguished eighteenth-century scholar Edward Gibbon had finished his *History of the Decline and Fall of the Roman Empire* in 1787, he wrote down the following words: "It was among the ruins of the Capitol, that I first conceived the idea of a work which has amused and exercised near twenty years of my life."

To speak of more recent times, there is Margaret Mitchell's great Civil War novel, *Gone with the Wind*. The first novel of a hitherto unknown young woman writer, it became overnight one of the most popular bestsellers of our time. Up to now, over eight million copies have been printed and sold; it has been made into a movie; it has been translated into many languages; and it has been produced as a book for the blind.

There have been many different and conflicting stories of how this book came to be written and how long it took. To find out the real facts I wrote to Mr. Stephens Mitchell, the author's brother (she herself died on August 16, 1949), and he was kind enough to answer my questions as follows:

"When the idea for *Gone with the Wind* first came to Mrs. Marsh (Margaret Mitchell) I do not know, for she wrote all of her life. She also had heard about the Civil War during her entire life, and had read books, articles, old diaries, old letters, on the subject from the time she began reading. She started

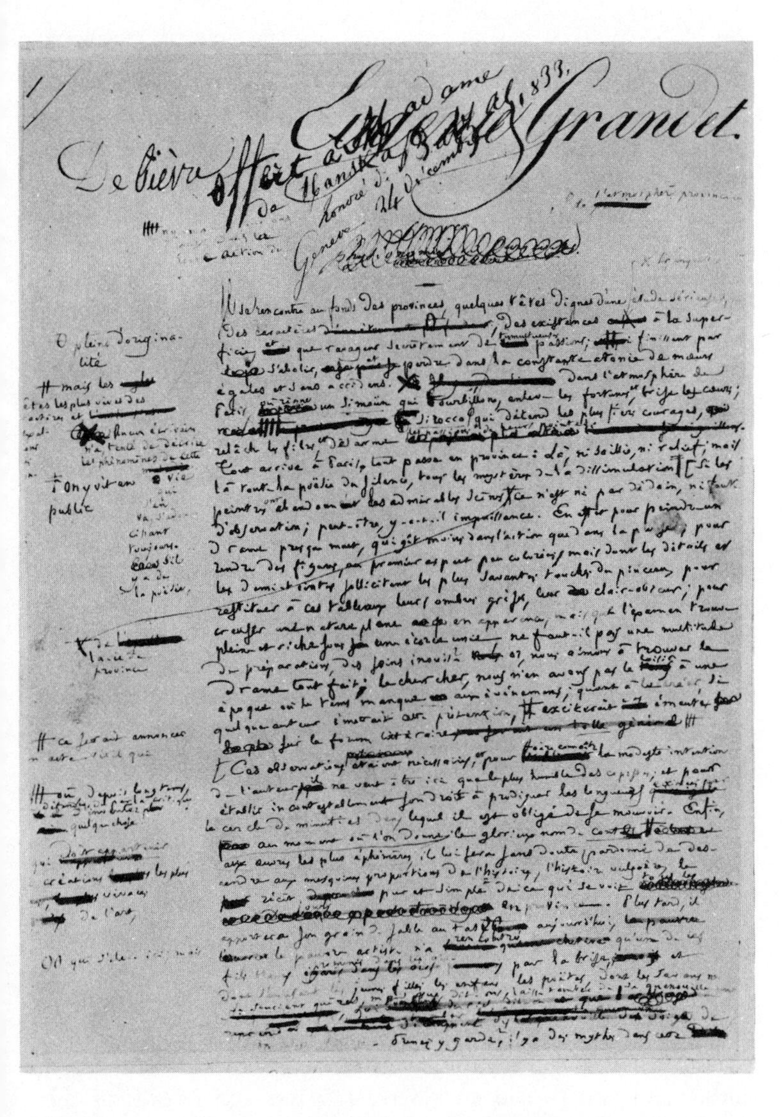

The first page of the original manuscript of Honoré de Balzac's *Eugènie Grandet*

writing on the book in 1926. The writing was intermittent during a period of ten years, for her family and personal life came first. Sometimes the better part of a year would go by without any work on it. She wrote the last chapter first, and when Macmillan (the publisher) first saw the manuscript, in April 1935, there was no first chapter. She wrote chapters separately, and wrote many drafts of each chapter, constantly checking and rechecking to perfect her work. In one of her letters she said, 'I had the story so completely in my mind that I was able to write the last chapter first and thereafter to skip about and work on any chapter I wished.'

"She re-worked the whole book during the thirteen-month period from April 1935 to May 1936. All of the early writing was done without reference to history books, so she did much research to satisfy herself as to the accuracy of manners, speech, and trueness to the time described. She had already labored to make her characters consistent, and now she double-checked on their ages, their peculiarities of speech, their names, and many, many other details of the book. The several versions of each chapter, though not different in story or plot, had to be selected, culled, and polished. This was a steady task, day by day and night by night."

After the book had appeared, Margaret Mitchell was once asked in a radio interview in Atlanta, her home town, how it happened that she, such a very modern person, knew her history so well. To this she answered:

"I grew up at a time when children were seen and not heard. That means that when I was a child I had to hear a lot about the Civil War on Sunday afternoons when I was dragged hither and yon to call on elderly relatives and friends of the family who had fought in the War or lived behind the lines. When I was a little girl, children were not encouraged to express their personalities by running and screaming on Sunday afternoons. When we went calling, I was usually scooped up onto a lap, told that I didn't look like a soul on either side of the family, and then forgotten for the rest of the afternoon while the gathering spiritedly refought the Civil War. I sat on bony knees, fat, slick taffeta laps and soft, flowered muslin laps. I did not even dare wriggle for fear of getting the flat side of a hair brush where it would do the most good. I should add, while I'm talking about knees and laps, that cavalry knees were the worst knees of all. Cavalry knees had the tendency to trot and bounce and jog in the midst of reminiscences and this kept me from going to sleep."

Not all books take so many years to prepare, needless to say. Some professional novel writers or authors of children's books manage to finish a book a year—at least for a while. Not all books turned out on a regular schedule are equally good. A first-class work is always something rare—even for our top-ranking authors!

Sometimes books have to be prepared in a hurry: when they are planned for a special occasion, for example. An important international conference, the opening of a great exhibition, or a sudden political development may offer a promising opportunity for a timely book dealing with the occasion. A record for speed was established by Pocket Books, publishers of inexpensive paper-bound books. They were able to prepare, print, and ship out to the bookstores a memorial volume on Franklin Delano Roosevelt within six days after his death on April 12, 1945.

Most books, I said, start as ideas in the head of an author. But that is not always the case. Sometimes it is the publisher, or his editor, who sees a promising opportunity for a book and goes out and finds a likely author to carry out his idea.

Nor are books always the work of a single man or woman. Two or more people may collaborate; sometimes an entire panel of experts may join forces, each contributing his own special knowledge and experience to the subject of the book. In these cases an editor is usually appointed to map out and guide the joint labor of the contributors.

Certain publications, such as important reference works, dictionaries, and encyclopedias may employ an entire staff of writers. The 1955 edition of the *Encyclopedia Britannica*, for instance, contains articles by no less than 4,829 experts.

Writing comes easy to some. There are authors who are able to dictate entire chapters to a secretary, a dictaphone machine, or even into the microphone of a tape recorder. Others can hammer out page after page on the typewriter. But to many, writing is a painfully slow and tedious process. It may mean long, lonely hours spent in a violent struggle with ideas and words. It may mean rewriting and rearranging, crossing out and putting back in again, for months or even years, until finally the writer is satisfied. The author wants to be sure he has given his words and sentences the greatest possible clarity, beauty, and forcefulness, so that they really express to the reader what he wants to say. Some of the finest books of all time are shining monuments of self-discipline, triumphs over fatigue, self-doubt, and even despair.

The question often arises: Can writing be taught and learned? The answer is: Yes, to a certain extent. There are writing courses in various schools, colleges, and universities; special seminars, summer conferences, and evening courses; and other, similar opportunities for professional training in writing. Here the young author can have his work reviewed and subjected to constructive criticism. A wise and experienced teacher can offer valuable advice and guidance. Meetings with young fellow-authors can be stimulating and helpful. But training and practice alone are hardly sufficient. Most people will agree that there has to be some natural talent. A strong urge for self-expression, the ability to recognize significant subject matter, a flair for language, and the capacity for long hours of hard work—these are the necessary prerequisites for a career in writing.

Why is it that people willingly undertake such an arduous task? There are, without question, many authors who simply have to write. Their creative drive is so strong that they cannot help themselves. But other considerations enter into the picture as well. There is, for instance, the desire to appear in public. Being an author makes some people feel important, and it's one way of getting some of the recognition which a person may have failed to earn for himself elsewhere. The laurels bestowed upon the great poet as upon a victorious athlete in ancient times have always stimulated competition. Curiously enough, no less than two thousand years ago, a writer of classical Rome made the sarcastic remark that some people write only because they want to see their own portraits painted in their books.

One of the most important reasons why people write books is, of course, to make a living or to increase their income. Authorship is a recognized and significant profession today.

This was not always the case. In all periods of history there have been great writers and great poets. Some of them have been very important people in their day, but not necessarily because of their writing, which they may have done only incidentally. Others were quite undistinguished in their professions and were remembered only because of their writing. In the first group one thinks of some great statesmen, the men who both make and write history, such as Caesar, Bismarck, and Winston Churchill. Herman Melville, on the other hand, who wrote the unforgettable *Moby Dick*, was an ordinary customs official. Wallace Stevens, one of the finest poets of his generation, was vice-president of a Hartford insurance company. Through the ages doctors and scientists have written, not only important books in their special fields, but also some distinguished works of literature.

To some great writers fame has come late in life, and sometimes even after death. John Keats, for example, was so discouraged by unfavorable criticism of his poems that he asked to have his tombstone engraved with the inscription: "Here lies one whose name was writ in water." Today he is considered by leading literary critics as the only English poet who can measure up to Shakespeare.

In bygone days most authors had a patron. He was an emperor, king, or nobleman or perhaps a high clergy-

Author and royal patroness

man, or a queen or princess. To this person the writer would dedicate his new book, and in return for this he would get some favor—money perhaps, or protection against enemies, or some kind of a job. To be mentioned in the dedication of a book by an important poet was something the great men of the world liked. It was, as we would call it today, "good publicity."

The gaining of influence, political power, or professional promotion is still one of the motivations of authorship, but in general financial reward is the return most writers expect from their efforts. However, it is really surprising how few authors can live solely on the income from their books. Each year from 11,000 to 12,000 new books and new editions are published in the United States, each in thousands of copies. (The total number of books sold in one year was counted officially in 1947, when it was found that more than 487 million copies of all kinds of books were sold.)

In spite of the large number of books published each year, and the many copies sold, it is not easy to make a living from writing books. There are very few people who earn a sufficient income from books alone. Many writers do get a steady yearly income from the sale of their books, especially if they publish regularly. But they usually have to get additional income from other sources. It takes some special good luck to "strike it rich" as a writer. If an author is fortunate enough to write a best-seller, if his book is translated into many languages (like *Gone with the Wind*), if his story is adapted for radio or television or for the motion picture screen, or reprinted in magazine form, then he can earn some really big money from his book.

Curiously enough, magazine writing pays much better than book writing, and there are quite a few men and women who make a good living that way. The reasons for this are not easily explained, but you will find some of the answers in the last chapter of this book.

Chapter 3

THE PUBLISHER

How does an author get his book published? He has to sell his manuscript. He must send a typewritten copy of his book to a publisher who he hopes will buy it. There is scarcely an author who has not had the disappointing experience of seeing his manuscript returned, sometimes a great many times, by different publishers, until finally he finds a publisher who has sufficient faith in his work to risk the cost of publishing it. Some very successful books, strangely enough, have had a hard time getting started. Publishers sometimes wish they had not refused a book when it turns out to be a wonderful success on the list of another publisher.

For instance, Edward Noyes Westcott's *David Harum*, the story of the noble small-town banker who cancels the poor widow's mortgage, was turned down by six well-known publishers in New York, Boston, and Chicago. It was finally accepted by D. Appleton & Co.

in New York in 1897 and published in September 1898. By February 1, 1901, over 400,000 copies of *David Harum* had been sold.

William de Morgan, author of *Alice-for-Short* (1907) and many other popular novels, had a very difficult time with his first novel. Again and again the bulky, handwritten manuscript bounced back onto his desk. At last a friend suggested that he get it typed. One day while she was typing the manuscript, the girl who had been assigned the job suddenly burst into tears. When the supervisor asked what was wrong, the typist cried: "I can't go on with this; it's too sad." This story reached the ear of a well-known publisher, who immediately declared that he would buy the novel, sight unseen.

Look Homeward, Angel, one of the greatest American novels of this century, was turned down by a number of publishers until its author, Thomas Wolfe, virtually despaired of ever seeing it in print. On the eve of his departure for Europe, he turned the manuscript over to Madeleine Boyd, a literary agent, who in September 1928 sent it on to Scribners. Their chief editor, Maxwell Perkins, recognized its extraordinary quality but wrote Thomas Wolfe that severe cutting and a vast amount of rearranging and rewriting would be necessary to turn the mammoth manuscript into a saleable volume. Wolfe agreed, and his collaboration with Perkins is one of the memorable cases of fruitful author-editor relationship.

When an author sends his manuscript, not directly to

a publisher, but to a literary agent, he entrusts it to a man or a woman who knows the book trade well and can save him time and needless disappointments. He or she is well acquainted with the policies and current programs of the various publishing houses and the interests and tastes of the editors who select books for publication. The agent, who gets a certain percentage of the author's income, can also be helpful in preparing the manuscript and working out the contract, which is a legal agreement between publisher and author. Payment is made either in a fixed sum or, more usually, in the form of royalties. Royalties are calculated as percentages on the retail price of a book.

The Authors Guild in New York City has worked out a "Basic Book Contract" as a guide for authors in their dealings with publishers. This model contract specifies that the author receives not less than 10% on the first 2,500 copies; 12½% on the next 2,500 copies; and 15% on all copies over 5,000. This means that if, for instance, the first novel of a young author, priced at $3.00, gets an exceptionally good start and sells, let us say, 3,000 copies in the first year, and another 2,500 in the second, he will have earned by then $1,912.50. However, in actual practice, the terms vary considerably. For instance, some publishers will not give 12½% until the first 5,000 copies have been sold, and so on.

Contracts are often signed before an author has completed his manuscript. In order to help him during the period of completion and to shorten the time of waiting until the book is printed and copies begin to sell, the author is usually given a guaranteed advance on his royalty, payable in part when the contract is signed and the balance when the manuscript is delivered to the publisher.

Royalties to authors, needless to say, make up only a part of a publisher's expenses. He has to maintain an expert staff of editors who help select manuscripts and prepare them for publication; a manufacturing department where the production of the books is planned and supervised; a sales force to sell the book to bookstores, libraries, and individual readers all over the country and abroad; a promotion and publicity department to spread the news of the new books he is publishing each season; a shipping department and all the other machinery necessary for an efficient business operation. He also has to pay for rent, electricity, and telephone, supplies, and many other items which make up what is called the "overhead" expenses.

Before he can make a profit on all the money he has invested in a single new title, many copies have to be sold. The publisher pays the advance against royalties, production costs (printing bills, etc.), advance advertising and promotion costs, before the books have been shipped, and before he collects any money for them. Only after the so-called "break-even point" is passed, meaning that enough copies have been sold to compensate him for the money advanced on any one book, does he begin to make a profit.

How many copies are printed at one time? Here is one of the big gambles of publishing, a question to which no one knows the correct answer. No matter how experienced a publisher and his staff may be, it remains at best a tricky game of guessing.

The decision depends very much on what kind of a book is being published. The volume you are now reading has been printed in a first edition of 5,000 copies. Some books come out in smaller editions. For instance, a highly specialized scientific work like David Bidney's *Theoretical Anthropology* was published by the Columbia University Press in an edition of about 2,500 copies. The same publisher's one-volume *Columbia Encyclopedia*, however, first published in 1935, has sold about 400,000 copies in two editions.

A novel by an unknown author will usually not come out in a very large edition. The publisher will rarely print more than 3,000 copies, but there is absolutely no assurance ahead of time that he can sell all or most of these copies. However, "optimism is an essential to trade book publishing," as one of my publishing friends once assured me. Sometimes, when special circumstances warrant this, a publisher will play for bigger stakes when bringing out a new author, and he may print up to 15,000 copies of a first novel.

A new novel by a well-established author like John Steinbeck, for example, will be printed by his publisher, the Viking Press, in about 100,000 copies (in which case the first and second printings are ordered simultaneously).

The greatest bestseller in the world is the Bible. No other book has been translated into so many different languages and has been printed in such large quantities since Johannes Gutenberg printed his Latin 42-line Bible between 1450 and 1455 in Mainz.

An edition of only one copy of a book was printed some years ago for Adolf Hitler. On his fiftieth birthday he was given by friends and admirers a history of the architecture of Old Berlin, with many beautiful reproductions of historic prints and drawings. The printer who was ordered to produce this publication pleaded for a larger edition. For practically the price of that one copy twenty-five or fifty copies could be produced and given or sold to libraries. The answer was "No. Only one copy!" Hitler's book was burned to ashes during the bombing of Berlin. Fortunately the printer, a courageous man who was not afraid of the Nazis, kept one copy for himself, which is the only existing copy of this book today. This, of course, is a very special case, a perfect example of the misuse of the printing press, making it serve not all the people, but the dictator only.

One group of books which require very large printings right from the start are the paper covers. We will discuss this in the chapter on Bookselling, page 159.

The extraordinary thing about book publishing is that publishers usually cannot stay in business on the income which they derive from the sale of the regular editions of their books alone. In this regard they are in the same boat as the author, who does not usually make a living from the straight sale of copies of the books he writes. Like him, the publisher needs the extra income that he receives from the sale of what is known as the "subsidiary rights." He is paid for granting permission for someone to translate the book into a foreign language, to reprint it in a magazine, to make it into a movie, radio, or television show, to reprint it for the members of a book club, and so on. The publisher shares these extra profits with the author.

Naturally, not all the books which a publisher selects in a particular season yield this kind of extra income. It is more likely to come in from the popular books on his list than from the more serious and scholarly ones.

There are quite a few publishers who see in their business not merely a way of making money but also a chance to make a contribution to society. They would like to discover a promising young author and support him through the difficult early stages of his career. They would like to print an occasional volume of worth-while poetry (which is rarely a profitable enterprise). There is experimental writing of one kind or another that should get a hearing, also books of high scholarly or artistic value which appeal to only very limited audiences. The publication of such books makes up what the publisher considers his cultural obligation, and this obligation is felt keenly in our finest publishing houses. Financially this is possible only if the unprofitable books are supported with extra income from the popular best-sellers, so that in some cases the sale of many copies of a book of indifferent literary merit makes possible the small edition of a volume which makes a valuable cultural contribution.

The idea of letting the income from popular hits pay for something of lasting value does not work only in publishing, but elsewhere as well. For example, there was a story in the *New Yorker* magazine (September 10, 1955) about the music-recording brothers Seymour and Maynard Solomon. Said Maynard:

> "My main love is and always has been Bach, and that's the prime reason I got into this business. You might think a good deal of Bach's music is on records, but there's only a fraction. Five years ago, when we started recording, under the name of the Bach Guild, there were well over two hundred Bach cantatas that had never been put on records. We've made a modest beginning by recording forty of them. Our jazz and popular records keep us going. One or two hits each year give us the capital we need for issuing Bach and other things we *like*."

While we are talking about the problems of publishing valuable books for small groups of readers, tribute should be paid to the remarkable achievement of university presses in this country. During the last half century there has been a spectacular rise in this kind of publishing all over the country. Before the year 1900 six or seven university presses had been started, not all of which survived into the twentieth century. But now, in mid-century, thirty or more such presses are in operation. This is a very significant movement. Not only are there now many more opportunities for the author of a serious work to get his book published, but these presses, located in many states of the Union, present also a valuable regional counterbalance against the almost complete concentration of what is called "trade publishing" in New York. "Trade publishing" is publishing for the general reader, as opposed to textbook publishing or scientific or medical publishing. In the eighteenth and nineteenth centuries, Boston and Philadelphia were more important, or at least as important, publishing centers as was New York City. There are still publishing houses in these cities, and in a few other places in various parts of the country, but most of the publishers are in New York City. Moreover, a good many who have their main office in other places maintain a small office in New York.

Occasionally, a book brought out by a university press can become as much of a publishing success as the popular bestseller of a trade publisher. For instance, Rachel Carson's wonderful study, *The Sea Around Us*, a perfect example of the scientific book that is also a work of art, sold well over one million copies in the first three years—1952–1955.

It is this element of chance which makes up much of the excitement of publishing. It is in some respects a superior kind of gambling, where the publisher, in a manner of speaking, risks his money on the performance of the authors in his "stable."

Every new manuscript arriving from the author is a fresh challenge to the skill of the publisher. His ability and experience can go a long way toward starting the book on its exciting journey to success.

Once a book has been accepted for publication and the contract signed, it must go through many steps before it finally reaches the reader. The first step is to prepare the manuscript for the printer, and that is the job of the editorial department. Here the book is checked for spelling and punctuation, for consistency of style, for accuracy of facts and quotations. The editor sometimes may wish to see changes made in the text which, in his judgment, will improve the book. For this the consent and the cooperation of the author are needed. Next comes the manufacturing process, which turns the manuscript into the printed book that thousands of people all over America and in many other countries can pick up and read.

Part II

HOW BOOKS ARE PRINTED AND DESIGNED

Chapter 4

HOW TO FIND OUT HOW BOOKS ARE MADE

When a publisher has bought a manuscript from an author, he must get it printed. He has to have many copies of the book ready for distribution to booksellers, libraries, and individual readers. In the publishing world of today this step is called the manufacturing process. It includes planning the physical form of the book, selecting paper and binding materials, setting up the type and preparing the illustrations, making plates for the printing press, printing the sheets, which are folded to make the pages of the book, and finally, binding, and wrapping the printed jacket around the finished book.

Perhaps you already know a little something about these steps, but there is a great deal more to it than is indicated in the few sentences which you have just read. The story of how books are made is really a very interesting one.

One very good way to learn more about this is to

visit a printing press or bindery. There one can see some of the processes in what is actually a complicated and long chain of operations. Such a visit is without question a worth-while experience which can be recommended to anyone interested in bookmaking and the graphic arts —but one should not go without some preparation. The reason it is important to know something about these machines ahead of time is that it is very difficult to see what they are actually doing. Very often, the really important things happen deep inside the machine where it is impossible for an onlooker's eye to penetrate. For this reason a photograph or motion picture of such a machine does not tell much about the actual operation.

We must understand that these machines have not been invented out of nothing. Each of them is the result of the ingenuity, the skill and experience of many generations of human beings. Some of the machines perform tasks today which started as single hand operations two thousand years ago!

If we wish to find out how books are made today, the best thing to do is to look at the way books were made in the olden days. This is a story not only of mechanical ingenuity, but also of man's overwhelming desire to communicate with his fellowman and a powerful testimony to his everlasting search for beauty.

There are three main stages in the story of bookmaking. First came the writing of books by hand, which lasted from around 3000 B.C. through the Middle Ages to the time, five hundred years ago, when printing with movable metal type was invented. This happened about half a century before Columbus discovered America. Next came the period of the early printed books, lasting about three hundred years. This stage ended with the dawn of the machine age, just around the time of the American Revolution—which was also the time when the Industrial Revolution got under way.

The third stage is the one we are still seeing today. It is very difficult to say how long it is going to last, and what the next great change is going to be.

Chapter 5

HANDWRITTEN BOOKS IN THE ANCIENT WORLD

Books came into being as a sort of insurance against the loss of memory. There was a time at the dawn of civilization when it was possible for the elders of the community to know by heart everything worth remembering and to pass it on to the next generation. Gradually, the oral traditions grew too voluminous for continuous memorizing. Collections of prayers and ritual; epics and sagas; the records of dynasties of kings and priests; compilations of laws; accumulated medical experience; and observations of the physical universe, of stars, seasons, and nature in its many forms made up the contents of books in the initial phase of their history.

At the start, single copies of a text were made and from them more could be copied as needed. The enormous rate of increase in the reproduction of a text in order to obtain many similar or identical copies of it is one of the most astounding aspects of the mechanics of our culture. In classical Rome as many as several hundred copies of the new work of a popular author could be produced in a relatively short time. In the same length of time the early printer was capable of producing several thousand copies. In the machine age books can be printed in millions of copies.

Writing, of course, is much older than the book. There were innumerable preparatory steps. Writing on a variety of perishable surfaces, such as vegetable fiber, cloth, and animal skin, was paralleled by the cutting of inscriptions, generally on stone, more rarely on metal, and also by stamping and pressing on clay. It is a matter of opinion whether we are justified in applying the term "book" to the clay tablets of ancient Mesopotamia. They contained collections of laws and some of the oldest poetry in the world, written, or rather pressed, into soft clay in so-called cuneiform, or wedge-shaped characters, and subsequently hardened. The most famous clay-tablet "book" is the ancient Sumerian *Gilgamesh Epos*, telling on a series of tablets the adventures of a great hero, and including an account of the Deluge.

No hesitation need be felt about applying the term "book" to the rolls of ancient Egypt, Greece, and Rome. The very name "volume," from the Latin word *volumen*, or roll, testifies to the connection of our books with the ancient scrolls. These rolls were the universally accepted media for communications of per-

Ancient papyrus rolls

manent value. They were produced and sold in multiple copies of standard size, and read and collected much as books are today.

Best known among the rolls of ancient Egypt are the *Books of the Dead*, prepared as burial gifts for departing souls, to guide them on their journey to the other world and to brief them for the judgment that awaited them.

The material of these and of most other ancient book rolls was papyrus, which grew abundantly in the delta of the Nile. The pith of the plant was cut into strips, laid crosswise in layers, pounded, and polished into smooth sheets which were joined into long continuous rolls. They were wound around a stick, the *omphalos* (Greek), *umbilicus* (Latin), or navel of the book. On the outside the rolls were protected by parchment wrappers or tubes, which were sometimes stained in accordance with a definite code, each color designating the major category to which the text belonged. To make sure that one might be able to identify a roll without having to unwind it, a tag or label of vellum with the name of the author and his work was attached.

In Roman times this was called the *titulus*—hence our "title." In the Greek and Roman rolls the columns of writing were placed side by side from left to right in continuous sequence. The original length of line or column width may be thought of as determined by one hexameter, which is the verse meter in which Homer's *Odyssey* and his *Iliad* were written. If you read a verse out loud, you will find that it contains just the amount of words you can say easily in one breath. Thus we can say that one lungful of spoken words equaled an eyeful of written words.

Very often, the book rolls began with the author's portrait. Illustrations in the ancient rolls were frequently scientific in nature, such as mathematical or astronomical diagrams and pictures of medicinal herbs. There is also evidence that some of the rolls containing the great epic poems of Homer and Virgil and the plays of Terence were illustrated. It is very possible that illustrations for

Homer and for some books of the Bible were painted on long continuous picture scrolls so that these stories would literally unfold before an audience in schoolroom and family circle—not unlike the images on motion picture or television screens today.

The oldest rolls were often of very great length, measuring from 50 up to 130 feet, and they came to be thought of as increasingly bothersome when the writing and reading of books and their use for reference purposes became a more general practice. In the time of Alexander the Great (356–323 B.C.), in the Hellenistic period, therefore, the old rolls were subdivided; hence the word "tome," from the Greek word for cutting. The work of an author would now consist of a number of rolls, frequently ten, which were kept as a unit in a special cylindrical container. Very likely such a process of physical separation and editorial subdividing was systematically practiced in the great libraries of the Ptolemies in Alexandria, where enormous quantities of papyrus rolls were collected and preserved between the third century B.C. and the fifth century A.D.

You may have heard the expression "a big book is a big evil," and perhaps you and your friends are in hearty agreement with this sentiment. The man who is supposed to have first said this lived 2,200 years ago, around 250 B.C. His name was Callimachus, and he was chief librarian of the Alexandrian library, author of a very important catalog of its treasures, and also a great Greek poet. The concentration of Greek volumes in the Alexandrian libraries, the largest accumulation of books ever undertaken up to that time, was a result of the great expansion of Greek civilization which followed the campaigns of Alexander the Great. Previously, the Greek city of Athens had been not only the intellectual center of the Western world, but also the seat of a book trade that was well organized and had a distribution system reaching to the outposts of Greek culture as far away as Southern France, Northern Africa, and the Near East.

Ancient Rome had a highly developed book trade. Papyrus rolls were now manufactured in standard grades of quality and in uniform sizes. Their length had considerable influence on literary composition. Duplication was by dictation or by copying from carefully prepared master copies. The book trade was concentrated in definite parts of the city. There were retail and second-hand stores, and the export business was brisk.

We know the names of some of the important ancient Roman publishers. Atticus, for instance, a cultured and learned gentleman, was Cicero's publisher. He owned many slaves, among them highly educated men and skilled copyists. Correspondence between Cicero and Atticus has survived. On one occasion, Cicero had discovered a painful error in the text of one of his new books. So he wrote to Atticus and demanded that he send a scribe around to all the places where copies were on sale and correct the error. Imagine Ernest Hemingway demanding the same thing of his New York publisher today!

Chapter 6

THE MEDIEVAL MANUSCRIPT

Important changes occurred in both the physical appearance and in the contents of books at the dawn of the Middle Ages. The traditional roll was abandoned for the "codex," which was a series of folded leaves protected by heavy wooden covers, the ancestor of the modern book. The transition from roll to codex was gradual; it extended over several hundred years. By the fourth century A.D. the process was completed. The change came about largely because of a growing impatience with the unavoidable inconveniences of the old book form. You could not open a book roll at more than one place at a time; it was hard to find something in a hurry; and back and forth reference was complicated and tedious. The increasing use of books in Christian church service, for instance, and in legal practice, hastened the change.

Some earlier writing experiments and materials were

From roll to codex

adapted to the new needs. The word "codex" originally designated a block or segment of wood. More particularly, the term had been applied to handy little notebooks in which two or more wooden tablets, covered with a writing surface of wax, were held together by rings, as in a modern looseleaf notebook. You wrote, or scratched (which is the original meaning of the word writing) with a sharply pointed instrument, the stylus, which had at the other end a flat little spatula for erasing,

The parchment maker

like the small eraser at the end of the modern pencil. Between the wooden boards of the codex, additional leaves were gradually inserted; usually these were made of parchment, which folded more easily and was more durable than the brittle and fibrous papyrus. Eventually only the two outer wooden boards were retained, which held between them the folded leaves sewn together at the back and attached to the covers by strong connecting thongs. Parchment had previously been used as a writing surface in the Near East; the book rolls of ancient Palestine and Persia, or the Dead Sea scrolls, were made of skins, either tanned as leather or bleached, stretched, and scraped as parchment or vellum (see illus. p. 55). The name parchment, or *Pergamenus*, is derived from the island of Pergamum, where King Eumenes II (241–197) founded a library in rivalry with the Ptolemies.

In the Far East, Chinese and Japanese books underwent the same change from rolls to folded leaves between covers, but the process of evolution was more simple and direct. The accordion-pleated book was a natural midway station, whereby a roll could be converted into a sequence of easily turned pages simply by folding. If you then stitched the leaves along one end, you had the simplest book form, a form which has survived in China and Japan from early times to the present day (see illus. p. 58).

Bookbinding originated in the Western world at the same time as the codex. It is thus a craft which antedates, by more than a thousand years, printing with

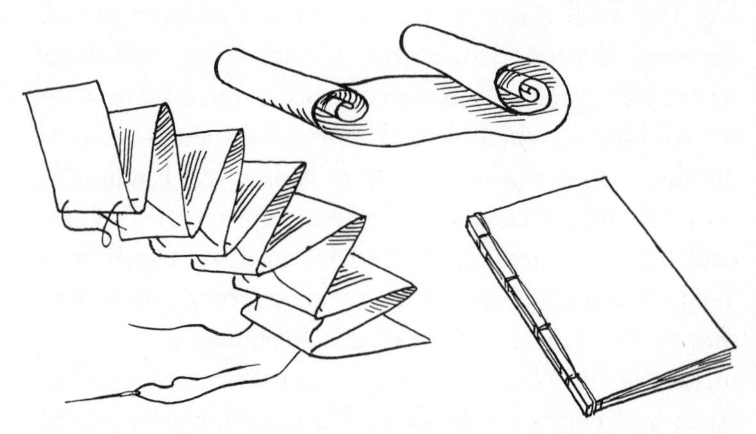

From Chinese scroll to Chinese book

movable type on a press. The heavy wooden boards, usually of seasoned oak, remained in universal use throughout Christendom until the Renaissance. They were the base on which decorations and covering were applied, often in exceedingly rich materials such as gold and silver worked by first-class craftsmen in a variety of goldsmith's techniques. The covers of these venerable volumes were often also studded with jewels and with cut stones arranged in the shape of the cross or of other Christian symbols (see page 59). Like the exquisite illuminations of the early Middle Ages, these precious bindings expressed the deep reverence felt by these artisans of long ago for their holy books.

For less distinguished volumes the bindings were not so elaborate and precious. Brown calf was the usual covering material, but this too was decorated, first by a

A medieval jeweled binding

simple but effective technique called blind-tooling, stamping without gold or color. Later on, more elaborate techniques of decoration were used. Gold tooling began to be practiced toward the beginning of the Renaissance. Most of the leather-decorating techniques came to Europe from the Arab world. The simplest of the medieval bindings were more or less flexible vellum covers. Through the Middle Ages, the backs remained unadorned and without identification marks. This will be more readily understood when one remembers that large accumulations of volumes were rare in medieval times. An individual scholar worked with half a dozen or a dozen volumes at his elbow, and libraries of a few hundred volumes were considered large ones. Therefore, the books were not kept standing on shelves as in a modern library, but lying flat on their sides on tables, or arranged side by side on reading desks. But then as now, books had their fixed locations in the library. One way of making sure that the volumes remained where they belonged and of protecting them against theft was to chain them to their reading desks.

Strangely enough, the medieval manuscript had no title page. It started with the *Incipit* ("Here beginneth"), followed by a brief identification of the contents. At the end came the *Explicit*, which means "Here is unfolded," or "Rolled out to the end," a term taken over from the rolls. Some of the early codices show clearly that they were copied from the roll. The famous Codex Sinaiticus in the British Museum, a fourth-century manuscript of the Bible, has four columns on each page. Today's familiar arrangement of one or two columns per page became customary at an early date.

A strict order of rank determined the amount, quality, and the arrangement of the decorations. At the beginnings of all major and many minor divisions and subdivisions in medieval manuscripts, we find splendid

THIS LINE IS SET IN ROMAN CAPITALS, ALSO CALLED UPPER CASE LETTERS

this line is set in lower case roman letters

This Line Is Set in Italic Upper and Lower Case Letters

THIS LINE IS SET IN CAPS AND SMALL CAPS

Capitals, lower case, italic, capitals, and small capitals, in 12 point Janson Linotype

ornaments and initial letters which both enhance the beauty of the page and help the reader to find his way.

To the modern reader, accustomed to comparatively few varieties of large and small Roman and Italic letters, the scripts used in medieval manuscripts give an impression of seemingly endless variety. Actually, the kind of writing encountered in a particular medieval manuscript is the result of an interesting combination of circumstances. It is determined in part by the deliberate choice

FORTESINVERIAN
PVLVERVLENTAC
ALSINONFVERIT

uossedu catmulti
enimuenientin
nominemeodice
tesquiaegosume

bere quasi suis meritas p̄su
mouendac transferend
sarias significant potest
atiquod in terduerunt, āq

dumdiocesesuisitat agebamus
nobisnescioquanecessitateremo
rantib; aliquantulum illepro
cesserat. Interim peraggerē
publicum plenamilitantib; uiris
fiscalis raedauen iebat. Sedubi

The evolution of handwriting

1. Roman square capital 2. Uncial 3. Half uncial

4. Carolingian minuscule

of a style of writing, in keeping with the nature of the text and with what was customary at a particular time in a particular community. But it is also determined by important changes in the basic structure of the Roman alphabet.

The early codex was written in formal capital letters only, as were the Greek and Latin book rolls. Informal, more hastily written, cursive Latin characters existed in classical Rome, but it was a long time before they were considered acceptable for books. It was not until the ninth century that, in the reign of the great Emperor Charlemagne, small letters or "minuscules" became universally accepted and standardized. It was from these Carolingian minuscules that the lower-case Roman letters of the early printers were derived, and they in turn are the antecedents of today's lower-case Roman letters. Our Roman capitals, like those of the early printers, stem directly from Roman inscriptions of the first centuries A.D.

The study of the various handwritings is called "paleography." It is a special skill to which some scholars devote an entire lifetime. The description in the above paragraph of what happened to the Roman alphabet is naturally a very sketchy one, and there is hardly room here for more than that. However, you might be interested in knowing a little more about this constant change in handwriting and the growth of new forms of letters. How did this really happen? The fascinating thing about it is that basically the change is the same as the one that our language undergoes all the time.

Every generation of human beings has the same influence on language: It likes to forget certain old-fashioned words and phrases and put some new ones in instead. All you need do is to read something written fifty or more years ago and to imagine how strange you would think it if someone actually spoke like that today. So, old-fashioned or obsolete words are gradually eliminated, and new words are gradually adopted. The spoken word of today is the written word of tomorrow and the printed word of the day after tomorrow, one might say.

In medieval handwriting, too, the older letter forms were gradually eliminated and more informal characters adopted instead. Like the new words accepted from

A medieval scholar at his writing desk

everyday speech into respectable written language, informal characters, which were developed in personal correspondence, business records, and so on, were gradually accepted into the more reserved and austerely regulated society of formal book letters. However, old letter forms were often purposely retained for special formal occasions and their very antiquity lent an air of traditional dignity to the document in which they appeared. A good example of this is the survival of the so-called "Old English" or "Black Letter" type, which is still used a good deal in religious printing in America today. These letters were not invented in England, nor are they typically German in origin, as some people believe. Actually, they are the result of a new style of medieval art, namely the Gothic style, which influenced every kind of artistic activity in practically every European country in the thirteenth, fourteenth, and fifteenth centuries. Letters became narrow and pointed with heavy strokes, hence the name "Black Letter." The column of script, too, became tall and narrow. The notion held by some students that this was done in order to save space and materials is contradicted by the splendid and generous margins, often filled with colorful ornamentation and illumination, of many Gothic manuscripts (see illus. p. 66).

Illustration played a very important role in medieval manuscripts. It was usually executed with a fine brush in brilliant colors, often on backgrounds of burnished gold. Some illustrations were drawn with pen and ink,

Formal Gothic book letter, pictorial initial "P", and marginal decorations, from a manuscript written c.1300 in Austria or Switzerland

and in the fourteenth and fifteenth centuries these were tinted with bright water colors.

The theme of medieval book illumination was primarily religious, scenes from the Bible, portraits of the Evangelists, and legends of the saints being the most frequent subjects. Very often scenes from the Old and the New Testament were arranged in pairs, so as to show the New Testament as the fulfillment of the prophecies of the Old.

From the thirteenth century onward, non-religious, worldly illustrations occupy an increasingly important place. Romances of chivalry, the heroic deeds of medieval knights, performed in honor of their ladyloves, the Arthurian legends, the poetry of the troubadours, or minnesingers, and descriptions of the more humble occupations of the peasants in the changing seasons of the year, are the themes of non-religious book illumination in the Middle Ages.

To see a beautiful medieval manuscript for the first time in one's life is a great experience. There are handwritten and hand-illuminated books surviving in which the glittering gold and the unbelievably clean and bright colors look as though they were painted only yesterday. Tightly pressed between the heavy wooden boards of the binding, the snow-white vellum leaves have rarely been exposed to sunshine, dust, or moisture. Not all the old manuscripts that still exist today are so perfectly preserved, but some great libraries and a handful of private collectors are the proud owners of such priceless treasures. The Pierpont Morgan Library and the New York Public Library, both in New York City, the Walters Art Gallery in Baltimore, the Free Library of Philadelphia, and the Houghton Library at Harvard University, for instance, are some of the places in the United States where beautifully illuminated manuscripts can be seen. Libraries in London, Paris, Brussels, Munich, Florence, Rome, and several other places in Europe also own such priceless manuscripts.

Like the study of medieval handwriting, the study of medieval illumination can well become the lifetime occupation of scholarly men and women. Every century saw new schools of great artistic significance come and go, from the unnamed Irish monks who illuminated the famous Book of Kells around the year 800 to the great artists in the Rhineland and northern France who worked for the Emperor Charlemagne in the ninth century; to the eleventh- and twelfth-century Benedictine monks in Monte Cassino, south of Rome; to the Parisian and English illuminators of the thirteenth century; to the fourteenth-century book painters in Florence, Bologna, Avignon, and Prague; and finally to the great fifteenth-century schools in Italy, France, and the Netherlands.

For someone living today, it is hard to understand that this great branch of medieval art was to a large extent practiced by artists who worked without pay. With the fall of the Roman Empire the highly organized book trade of classical Rome had shrunk nearly to the

Miniature portrait of a medieval scholar, painted into initial "S", from a 14th-century Italian manuscript

vanishing point. Non-commercial book production took its place. The fact that manuscript-copying became one of the important duties of monastic life in the Western world had far-reaching consequences for the transmission of our culture. The copying of the works of those classical authors whose writings were considered important contributions to the Christian tradition insured their preservation. Bible texts and commentaries, liturgical books, the works of the Church Fathers, and the teachings of the great Christian philosophers and of the founders of various monastic orders formed the core of monastic manuscript production. In the great medieval scriptorium, or writing room, the combined labors of important theologians, of highly skilled scribes, and of illuminators of great artistic ability produced books of unrivaled dignity and beauty. These manuscripts did not necessarily stay in the communities where they were made. The great masterpieces were usually created for an important patron—an emperor, a king or a queen, a Prince of the Church, or a duke. A certain amount of traffic in books existed among various houses of a religious order, where loans, exchanges, and gifts occurred.

A shift in the function of medieval books and in readership became apparent from about the thirteenth century onward. A new interest in science and philosophy, the rise of modern languages and literature, the new flowering of chivalrous poetry, the early reawakening of classical studies, and the rise of popular education, both religious and secular—all these factors quickened the pulse of medieval book production. In the newly emerging European universities we find the growth of a secular book trade. The stationer, under strictest editorial and economic supervision from his academic authorities, kept a prescribed stock of basic textbooks from which he made copies for sale, or lent out sections for students to copy. Other secular manuscript workshops were started by notaries, scribes, and schoolmasters, to produce inexpensive paper manuscript copies of popular romances and histories. Their activities can be looked upon as the earliest roots of modern bookselling and publishing.

It is important to recognize that all this happened before Gutenberg's invention of printing with movable metal type on a wooden press. The growing demand for

Secular scribes in a 15th-century manuscript workshop

inexpensive books in a larger number of similar copies than was hitherto customary was recognized outside the monasteries. Enterprising townsmen called upon the services of non-religious scribes and illustrators, organized in various guilds, to start workshops for the copying of inexpensive paper manuscripts of popular reading matter. The Church, too, found means now for encouraging the production of popular religious books, many of them outright picture books in bright colors, such as the *Poor Man's Bible*, or the *Mirror of Human Salvation*.

Chapter 7

THE INVENTION OF PRINTING

The greatest single event in the history of the book was the invention of printing from movable metal type. Here was a radically new method for the quick and inexpensive duplication of books. The tedious labors of the scribe were replaced by the printing press. In the same time in which one copy of a text was written by hand, hundreds or even thousands of copies could now be printed. This happened at the dawn of the modern age, and it made it possible for the book not only to maintain its inherited central position in Western culture, but also to make great contributions in a period of tremendous growth and rapid expansion of education. In five centuries of tremendous scientific discovery and technical progress, during social developments which had a profound effect upon the fate of the human race, and in ever-widening areas of communication, the printed book was able to render invaluable services to mankind.

The changes resulting from the invention of printing were not immediately visible. The tremendous power of the printing press, to spread current information and fresh ideas by word and picture much more quickly and to many more people than ever before, was not discovered at once. At first the press seemed chiefly a new medium for the reproduction of already existing texts, for the vast body of Christian religious writing, and for the works of the ancient Greek and Roman authors, and also the accumulated wisdom of the Arab world. That printing could be an instrument which might change people's minds and cause them to take specific action was not recognized for quite a while. Also, it took a whole century for the printed book to develop a form of its own which was no longer dominated by the artistic traditions of the medieval manuscript. The goal which the earliest printers saw before them was the speedier production at much lower prices of the kind of books already in existence in handwritten form.

The central figure in the invention of printing was Johannes Gutenberg, member of a noble and influential family of Mainz on the Rhine. Early in his life (we do not know just when) he must have conceived the fundamental idea for his great invention. He spent many years in what must have been a most exasperating period of trial and error, experimenting, rejecting the impractical, improving the possible. His efforts were crowned by the deep satisfaction of seeing his boldest dreams come true, but the satisfaction was tempered by the ever-present worry over insufficient funds and, finally, by personal failure in business. But the memory of this great man shines through the ages. At least once every century (in 1540, 1640, 1740, 1840, and 1940) printers and booklovers throughout the world have honored Johannes Gutenberg and his invention.

He was active in Strassburg and Mainz and perhaps

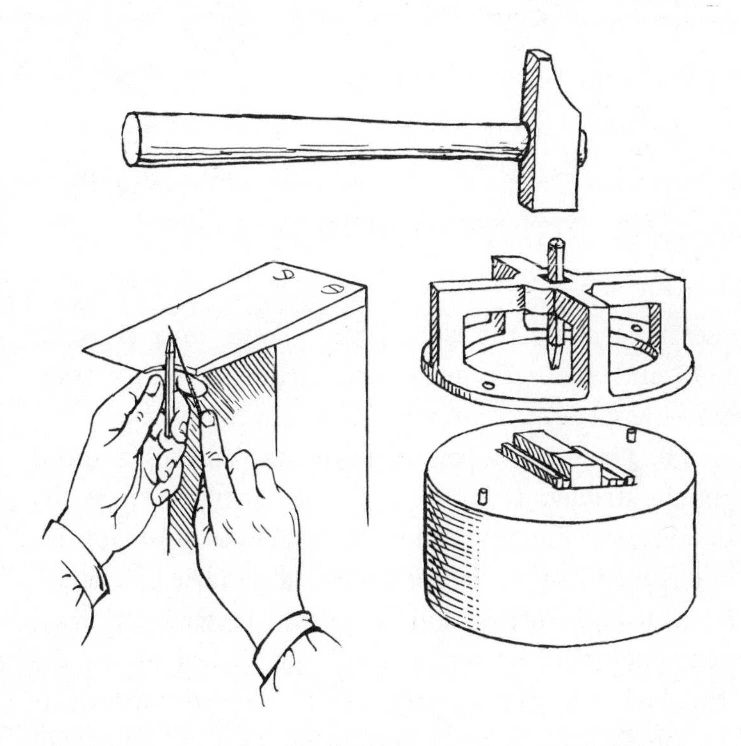

How type is made. I: Engraving the punch and striking the matrix

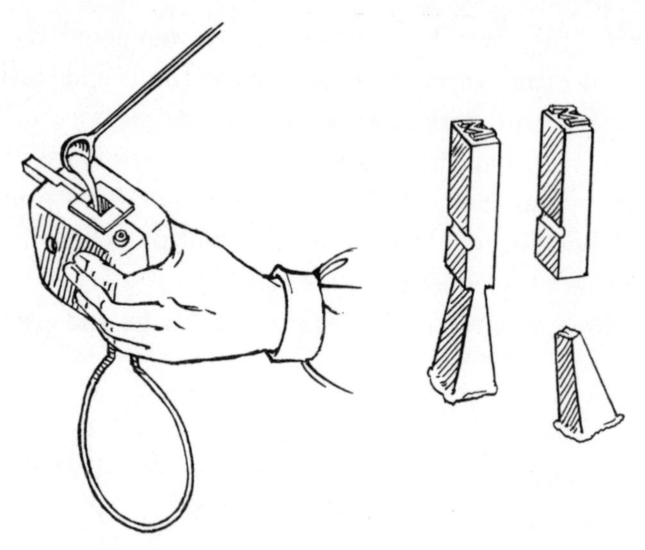

How type is made. II: Casting type in the mold

elsewhere along the river Rhine. Some time between 1430 and 1460 this man succeeded in printing from movable metal type on a wooden printing press.

He created his printing type by cutting a metal punch, striking from it a so-called matrix (from the Latin *mater*, meaning "mother"), and casting from this in a special casting mold the desired number of characters. Of equal height and on a truly rectangular shaft, this type could be set by hand and locked up on the level bed of a printing press, which yielded impressions on moistened sheets of handmade paper showing an evenness and beauty rarely rivaled by later printers.

The steel punch, as you can see, is the important

starting point. There is a simple little experiment you can carry out if you would like to see how it works. The idea is to get a letter, or, better for your purpose, any simple design like a heart or a star, cut into the tip of a shaft. Naturally, you cannot cut into steel, but a potato will do just as well for this particular experiment. So take a potato and cut it into the shape of a pyramid with a flat top. Into this top cut your design, or rather, carve away everything except the design. If you let the potato dry you can spread out some oil color (or printing ink, if you can get hold of some), stamp the potato into it and then onto a piece of paper. You can repeat the impression and arrange it into patterns. You can use two

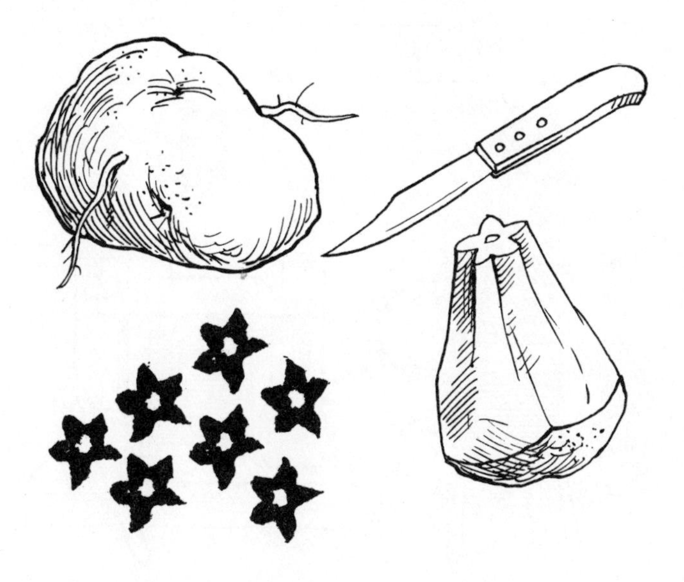

How to make a potato print

different stamps alternately; also, more than one color can be used to make a potato print.

If you try this, you will be surprised at the variety of attractive pattern papers you can make with very simple materials. The whole experiment need not take more than an hour or so.

Gutenberg did not have to create all the elements of his typographic invention. Paper had been introduced into Europe from the Orient at least 250 years earlier. The basic principle of ancient paper-making consists in

The paper maker at work

What paper and printed letters look like under a microscope

breaking down by continuous beating various kinds of cloth remnants—silk, linen, cotton, etc.—into individual fibers. Fermentation is also employed in the decomposition of the fibers to form the so-called pulp, a watery substance of milky appearance, in which the fibers float. This pulp is stirred into big wooden containers called vats. Into these, the vatmen dip rectangular frames covered with a thin net made of bamboo (in the Orient) or wire (in the West). By shaking out the water the pulp is caused to settle on the surface of these molds, where the interlocking fibers form the sheet of paper. This is then pressed down onto a piece of felt, put in a press to remove the excess water, and finally hung up on a line to dry like laundry. With certain changes and improvements the old Chinese way of making paper remained the same until the end of the eighteenth century.

Block printing, too—a primitive form of printing from solid wooden planks without the aid of a printing press—had come from China, and it had been used in Europe for textile printing, for the making of playing cards, and for single broadsides carrying the images of various saints. The use of a number of such woodblocks, each with pictures and text, to make so-called block-books, printed by the simple process of rubbing, was first being practiced simultaneously with Gutenberg's experiments.

Gutenberg was not the only man who was working toward printing with movable type. There is evidence

A Chinese woodblock printer at work

tunicam tuā tollere dimitte et palliū:
et quicunq3 te angariauerit mille pas-
sus: vade cū illo et alia duo. Qui aūt
petit a te da ei: et volenti mutuare a te
ne auertaris. Audistis quia dictū ē:
diliges pximū tuū · et odio habebis
inimicū tuū. Ego aūt dico vobis dili-
gite inimicos vestros: benefacite hiis
qui oderūt vos · et orate pro psequēti-
bus et calūniantib3 vos: ut sitis filij
patris vestri qui in celis est · qui solem
suū oriri facit super bonos ⁊ malos:
et pluit sup iustos et iniustos. Si enī
diligitis eos q̄ vos diligūt: quā mercedem habebitis? Nōne et publicani
hoc faciūt? Et si salutaueritis fratres
vros tātū: qd̄ āplius facitis? Nōne ⁊
ethnici hoc faciūt? Estote ergo vos pfe-
cti: sicut ⁊ pater vester celestis pfect9 ē. VI
Attendite ne iusticiā vestrā facia-
tis corā hominib3 ut videami-
ni ab eis: alioquin mercedem nō habebitis apud patrem vestrū qui in celis ē.
Cū ergo facis elemosinā noli āte te tu-
ba canere: sicut ypocrite faciūt ī synagogis et in vicis ut honorificēt ab hominibus. Amen dico vobis: receperūt
mercedē suā. Te aūt faciēte elemosinā:
nesciat sinistra tua quid faciat dextra
tua: ut sit elemosina tua ī abscōdito: ⁊
pater tuus qui videt ī abscondito reddet tibi. Et cum oratis: non eritis ypocrite qui amāt in synagogis et in an-
gulis plateaꝝ stantes orare: ut vide-
antur ab hominibus. Amē dico vobis: receperūt mercedē suā. Tu aūt cum
oraueris intra ī cubiculū tuū: ⁊ clauso
ostio ora patrem tuū in abscondito: ⁊
pater tuus qui videt in abscōdito reddet tibi. Orantes aūt nolite multum
loqui: sicut ethnici faciūt · putant enī:
q9 in multiloquio suo exaudiantur.
Nolite ergo assimilari eis. Scit enim
pater vester quid opus sit vobis: an-
tequā petatis eum. Sic ergo vos ora-
bitis. Pater noster qui es in celis san-
ctificetur nomē tuū. Adueniat regnū
tuū. Fiat volūtas tua: sicut in celo et
in terra. Panē nostrū supsubstāciale
da nobis hodie. Et dimitte nobis de-
bita nostra: sicut et nos dimittimus
debitoribus nostris. Et ne nos indu-
cas in temptationē: sed libera nos a
malo. Si enim dimiseritis hominib3
peccata eoꝝ: dimittet et vobis pater
vester celestis delicta vestra. Si autem
non dimiseritis hominibus: nec pater vester dimittet vobis pccā vestra.
Cū aūt ieiunatis: nolite fieri sicut ypocrite tristes. Extermināt enī facies suas:
ut pareant hominibus ieiunantes.
Amen dico vobis: quia receperunt
mercedem suā. Tu autem cū ieiunas
unge caput tuū et faciē tuā laua: ne
videaris hominibus ieiunās sed pa-
tri tuo qui est in absconso: et pater tuus qui videt in absconso reddet tibi.
Nolite thesaurizare vobis thesauros
in terrā: ubi erugo et tinea demolitur:
et ubi fures effodiūt et furantur. Thesau-
rizate aūt vobis thesauros ī celo: ubi
nec erugo nec tinea demolit: ⁊ ubi fures nō effodiūt nec furātur. Ubi ē the-
saur9 tu9: ibi ē ⁊ cor tuū. Lucerna corpo-
ris tui ē oculus tu9. Si oculus tu9 fuerit simplex: totū corp9 tuū lucidū erit.
Si aūt oculus tuus fuerit neq3: totū
corpus tuū tenebrosum erit. Si ergo
lumē qd̄ in te est tenebre sunt · ipe tenebre quāte erūt? Nemo potest duobus
dn̄is seruire. Aut enim unū odio habe-
bit ⁊ alteꝝ diliget: aut unū sustinebit
et alteꝝ contemnet. Non potestis deo
seruire et mamone. Ideo dico vobis:

A page from the Gutenberg Bible

that elsewhere in Europe experiments were carried on. It is impossible to say today what their connection, if any, may have been with Gutenberg's experiments in Strassburg and Mainz. One thing is certain: it was in Mainz, between 1450 and 1455, that the magnificent 42-line Bible was created, which marks the emergence of the art of printing from the experimental stage. It was in Mainz that Gutenberg's former associates and later his successors, Johannes Fust and Peter Schoeffer, produced the first great books to be used for divine service in the churches, with the decorations ingeniously printed in several colors. It was from Mainz that this new art of printing spread down the river Rhine to Cologne, the Netherlands, and England; up the river to Strassburg, Basel, and beyond to Lyons and the Iberian Peninsula, west to Paris, and across the Alps to Italy, and on to the whole of Europe and eventually all over the world.

Chapter 8

EARLY PRINTED BOOKS

There is something very special about a book printed in the fifteenth century, a peculiar beauty and strength and at the same time something primitive, which sets it apart from all books printed later on. A book printed in the fifteenth century is called an "incunable," from the Latin word for swaddling band or cradle, indicating that it was made during the infancy of printing. A typical incunable is a thick, large book, bound in blind-stamped calf over wooden boards. Unlike a modern book it has no title page, but the first page of the text is often finely decorated with an elaborate illuminated border and initial letters. Ornamental initial letters and other decorations appear also throughout the text. An incunable ends with the colophon, a printer's note on the last page, which usually reveals the place and date of printing and the name of the printer.

An astonishing variety of different kinds of printing

types (also called typefaces) was used in the early books, reflecting the even greater variety of manuscript hands. The Gothic types included large formal letters, used mainly for liturgical volumes, smaller letters for various scholarly works, and cursive type based on the current everyday handwriting of the various European communities. They were used for story books which were no longer written in medieval Latin, but in English, German, French, Italian, and Spanish. Thus many books written in the spoken languages of the time were printed in types closely resembling the everyday handwriting of the time. William Caxton, England's first printer, used these types for his editions of Chaucer and other important milestones of early English literature.

Roman typefaces, the ancestors of our current everyday types, were cut by many printers, especially in Italy, from a beautiful clear hand developed by the humanistic scholars and artists of the early Renaissance. It was in Venice that the most successful Roman letters were created and the name of the printer Nicolaus Jenson is best known in this connection.

The most frequent form of illustration in the early printed books was direct and often very simple storytelling by means of woodcuts in primitive but strong outlines, gradually developing into richer and more complicated patterns. A woodcut was made—and is still made today—by first drawing the lines that make up the picture on the smooth surface of a piece of fairly soft wood, such as cherry or peartree wood. As on your

Meditatione como leuandose lo signore Ie-
su da la oratione uenne in contro a Iuda
& a le turbe che ueniuano per pigliarlo·
& como fu preso & del tagliar de la ore-
chia facto pietro./

PArlando lo benignissimo maestro
cũ li chari discipuli & reprehendẽ-
dogli de la somnolentia ecco Iuda ueni-
re da la longa/ hauendo seco la turba de
li ministri la quale haueua tolta da li

ut relictũ putes. A. Ego uero:& quidem fecit etiam iste
ie epilogus firmiorem. M. Optime inquam. Sed nunc
uidem ualitudini tribuamus aliquid. Cras autẽ:& quos
ies erimus in tusculano agamus hæc: & ea potissimum:
uæ leuationem habeant ægritudinum:formidinum:cu-
iditatum:qui omni e philosophia ẽ fructus uberrimus.

ARCI TVLLII CICERONIS TVSCVLA-
NARVM QVAESTIONVM LIBRI .I. FINIS.

Italian humanist minuscule writing (above) and Nicolaus Jenson's roman type (below)

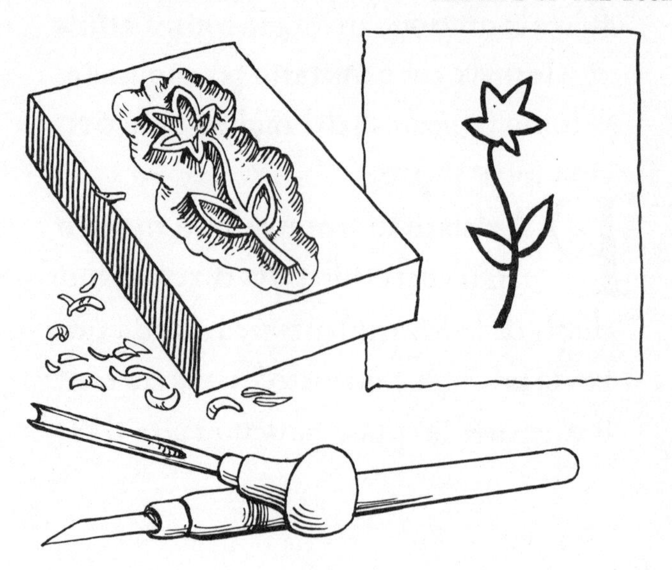

How a woodcut is made

potato, everything is then cut away from the surface except the lines of the drawing; they should now stand out in relief, like ridges of narrow mountains rising from a plain.

If you want to try this, a good idea would be to do this first with a piece of linoleum pasted on wood, which you can get at an art supply store. Any sharp pocket knife can be used, but there are special knives which can be bought for this purpose. Next, the surface of the lines is inked with ink balls. Today we use rollers for this, which pick up a film of spread-out ink from a smooth stone or glass plate. Next, you place a piece of clean white paper over it (a fairly soft paper with a

1. A late 14th-century woodcut of St. Dorothy

2. From Thomas Lirer's *Suebian Chronicle*, 1486

3. Woodcut of a teacher and his students, 1492

4. The month of August, from *Compost et Calendrier des Bergères*, 1499

Examples of early woodcut illustrations

natural finish is best for this purpose). It is best to avoid hard and brittle paper, like bond paper, and also the shiny sheets of paper which are coated with a special glossy finish. Then, you put the woodcut and paper under the platen of a printing press and press the platen down, so that the ink is transferred from the woodcut to the paper. This is called "pulling" or "taking" an impression. To make a print without a press, you can take a spoon and rub the paper hard in an even circular motion. It takes some practice to do this.

German and Dutch woodcut artists furnished some

A 15th-century printing establishment. I: Type casting, type setting, proofreading, and press work

of the most characteristic and forceful of the fifteenth-century illustrations, while French work added a fanciful and sometimes bizarre note of its own. Italian woodcuts, which appeared relatively late on the scene, exhibit a special graceful charm.

The workshop of a fifteenth-century printer was usually small, and he did a great many jobs himself. Very often he made his own printing type; he was his own press builder, printer, editor, publisher, and bookseller. Only gradually was there a division of labor. Binding and papermaking, of course, were established crafts long

A 15th-century printing establishment. II: Bookselling

before the printer appeared on the scene. In addition, type founding (the making of printing type) and especially bookselling and publishing gradually became separate trades. Relatively early, competition and other economic factors favored the growth of farflung networks of book distribution. Gutenberg's former disciple, Peter Schoeffer of Mainz, for instance, developed a series of trading posts manned by permanent agents, not only in Germany, but also over much of France. Anton Koberger, a famous printer of Nuremberg, had agents in Switzerland, France, and Spain.

Not very many copies of a book were printed in the early days, a few hundred being the rule. Occasionally very popular books appeared in editions of one or two thousand copies. Books which had already circulated in manuscript form for many generations and were well established with certain groups of readers predominated at first. Gradually, however, current works by new authors came to be written especially for distribution in printed form, and current events and the clash of opinions found prompt expression in print. Nothing so much favored the change of printing from an early tool of manuscript reproduction into a powerful medium of current communication as the great religious controversy between the Protestant and the Catholic Church.

Chapter 9

FROM THE RENAISSANCE TO THE INDUSTRIAL AGE

It was in sixteenth-century Italy that the printed book emerged from the experimental stage and found a form of its own which lasted for the next three centuries. This new form expresses very firmly and very beautifully the spirit of a new age—the Renaissance.

What do we mean when we speak about the spirit of an age? We mean the ideas and beliefs which dominate the minds of people living at a certain time. We mean the discoveries and the dreams, the experiences of the body and the soul, the hopes and fears, which grow so strong and last so long that they find expression in the things created by man.

In the Middle Ages, for instance, in the period of Gothic art from the twelfth to the fifteenth century, there was a powerful unity of religious purpose and form. It pervaded the whole devotional life of the communities.

While the words of the Gospel were read out in Latin from beautifully illuminated manuscripts, with their gilded initial letters reflecting the light of the candles around the altar, the sun would filter through the tall stained-glass windows on which scenes from the Bible were depicted. Paintings on the High Altar and in the many chapels, and frescoes on the walls of the cloisters, told the story of Old Testament prophecy and New Testament fulfillment through the life and the deeds of Christ.

To the masses who knew no Latin or Greek, these picture sequences were mighty textbooks in monumental format which they could read and understand.

The great change which took place in the Western world at the end of the Middle Ages was the rediscovery of the spirit of classical antiquity, which replaced the powerful influence of Gothic art as an expression of medieval Christianity. This did not mean that the people of Europe abandoned the Christian faith, but that they rediscovered a lost world. This is what is meant by the word "Renaissance"—rebirth. Men and women saw with new eyes the remains of the buildings and the sculpture of ancient Greece and Rome. They tried to resurrect in their own new buildings the beauty which they discovered in the ruins. They found a fresh joy in reading Homer and Virgil and all the other classical authors. They modeled their philosophical thinking and their scientific research on the ancient authors. Through them they discovered once again that one could live in direct contact with nature.

For the first time in many hundreds of years the artists began to draw, paint, and model from nature instead of copying from model books or from each other. The artist and the scientist together discovered the nude human body, its beauty and its anatomical structure. The birds, beasts, and flowers were now drawn from nature and carefully described by the naturalist. Astrology began to turn into Astronomy, Alchemy into Chemistry. Courageous travelers began to venture far out from the known lands and shores into the unexplored seas. The search for a westward passage to India led to the discovery of America. All these new interests and discoveries were promptly and faithfully reflected in both the contents and the physical appearance of the books of the Renaissance period.

Seven years after Columbus first set foot on American soil in 1492, there appeared in Venice in 1499 one of the most beautiful books ever to be printed. It had a long and complicated name, the *Hypnerotomachia Poliphili,* a curious sort of novel by Francesco Colonna. This book is considered to be one of the most successful expressions of the idea of classical beauty and harmony in book art. It was the work of the great Italian scholar-printer Aldus Manutius.

Aldus made many important contributions to the progress of book production. He was greatly interested

Woodcut from Francesco Colonna's *Hypnerotomachia Poliphili*, 1499

in printing attractive and correct editions of Roman and Greek authors. His experience in the designing of a Greek type of great delicacy and firmness paved the way for the creation of Italic printing type, which he was the first to use. This in turn made possible the production of a series of pocket-sized editions of the classics, the first significant step on the road toward handy, inexpensive books of permanent value for an ever-growing circle of book readers. Aldus was also among the first to introduce a new and lighter material for the cover of

SATYRA

H ic libros dabit, & forulos, mediamq; Mineruam,
Hic modium argenti, meliora, ac plura reponit
P ersicus orborum lautissimus, et merito iam
S uspectus, tanquam ipse suas incenderit ædes.
S i potes auelli circensibus, optima Soræ,
A ut Fabrateriæ domus, aut Frusinone paratur,
Q uanti nunc tenebras unum conducis in annum:
H ortulus hic, puteusq; breuis, nec reste mouendus,
I n tenues plantas facili diffunditur haustu.
V iue bidentis amans, et culti uillicus horti,
V nde epulum possis centum dare Pythagoreis.
E st aliquid quocunque loco, quocunque recessu,
V nius sese dominum fecisse lacertæ.
P lurimus hic æger moritur uigilando, sed illum
L anguorem peperit cibus imperfectus, et hærens
A rdenti stomacho. nam quæ meritoria somnum
A dmittunt? magnis opibus dormitur in urbe.
I nde caput morbi redarum transitus arcto
V icorum inflexu, & stantis conuitia mandræ
E ripiunt somnum Druso, uitulisq; marinis.
S i uocat officium turba cedente uehetur
D iues, et ingenti curret super ora Liburno,
A tque obiter leget, uel scribet, uel dormiet intus,
N anque facit somnum clausa lectica fenestra,
A nte tamen ueniet, nobis properantibus obstat
V nda prior, magno populus premit agmine lũbos
Q ui sequitur, ferit hic cubito, ferit assere duro
A lter, at hic tignum capiti incutit, ille metretam.
P inguia crura luto, planta mox undique magna
C alcor, et indigito clauus mihi militis hæret.

The Aldine italic, as used by Aldus Manutius in his 1501 Juvenal edition

books, namely cardboard, which gradually replaced wood.

The Renaissance saw many significant changes in the exterior and interior appearance of the book. While pigskin and vellum continued to be used as binding materials for at least another century and a half, and while calf's leather lasted well into the nineteenth century, an important new introduction was goatskin, called "morocco," from its main region of origin in North Africa. From the Islamic world, too, came the use of gold for exterior decoration, combined with the traditional method of blind-stamping into the new art of gold tooling, and the use of intricate and colorful leather inlay techniques. These were used not only in Italy but also on the fine bindings of great French bibliophiles such as Jean Grolier and Thomas Mahieu, or Maioli.

Some of the decorations cut on binders' stamps were transferred to type punches and from these were cast the so-called "fleurons" or printers' flowers, used as single ornaments or gracefully combined into title page borders, and decorations used at the beginnings and ends of chapters. This form of ornamentation has remained popular to the present day.

At just about the time when printers' flowers began to be used for adornment, woodcut decoration and illustration began to decline. During the first century of printing the woodcut had developed from primitive beginnings and limited functions into a medium of great

1. A 15th-century German binding, blind-stamped in calf

2. A 16th-century gold-tooled morocco binding made for Jean Grolier

3. A royal 18th-century French binding in red morocco

4. A 20th-century German binding in red, black, and yellow morocco, made by Ignaz Wiemeler

Examples of decorated leather bindings

Woodcut by Albrecht Dürer, from the *Revelations of St. Brigid*, 1502

artistic strength and one useful for many purposes. Among the great artists who used the woodcut were Dürer and Holbein in Germany, Bernard Salomon and Geoffroy Tory in France, and many other artists, known and unknown, in Italy and elsewhere. In their hands, book illustration reflected not only the striving for harmony and beauty, but also man's struggle for an understanding of his position in the world around him, and his search for the ultimate values. The woodcut also served magnificently as a record of the newly discovered physical universe. Almost all the first great illustrated books in the natural sciences and medicine, in cartography and technology, were illustrated by woodcuts. After the middle of the sixteenth century copper engraving, soon followed by etching, and eventually by a host of similar processes, triumphed over the woodcut.

The introduction of copper engravings had a very decided effect on book design. In order to understand this, we should know a little more about this interesting picture-printing method. It is different from the kind of printing you have read about so far.

All printing methods have one thing in common, a thing which in fact could be called the very essence of

"Death and the money changer," woodcut from Hans Holbein's *Dance of Death*

the technique of printing: the printing surface, from which the printer transfers ink on to paper, is prepared in such a way that when the ink is applied, it automatically is deposited on those parts of the plate which are supposed to print, and it is automatically kept away from the parts which should not print.

In printing from type—which the modern printer calls "letterpress" printing—the ink is deposited on top of the letters, which stand out in relief above the surface of the block.

For this reason letterpress printing is classified as a *relief process.* Woodblock and linoleum-block printing are also called relief processes. They all have in common the fact that the ink is deposited on top of the printing surface (like an elevated railroad), and from there it is pressed into the paper, making a little indention in it.

There are two other basic processes: one is the *intaglio process*, meaning literally the "cut-in" process, where the ink is deposited into a groove cut into the surface of the printing plate (like a subway with the covering surface removed). In printing, this leaves a little elevation on the paper, which you can actually feel with your finger.

The third basic process is called the *planographic process*, in which the ink is placed level with the surface of the printing plate (like a streetcar). Since this process came into use several centuries later than relief and intaglio printing, we will not discuss it until later.

Copper engraving is the oldest of all intaglio proc-

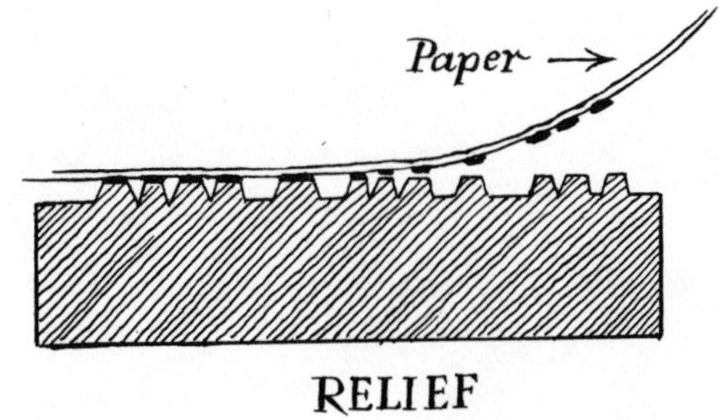

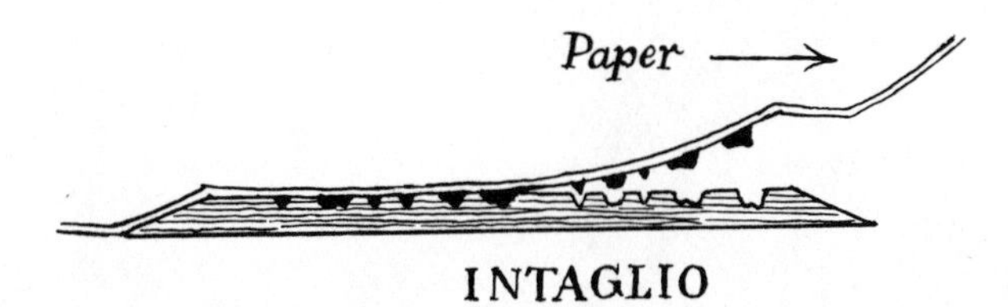

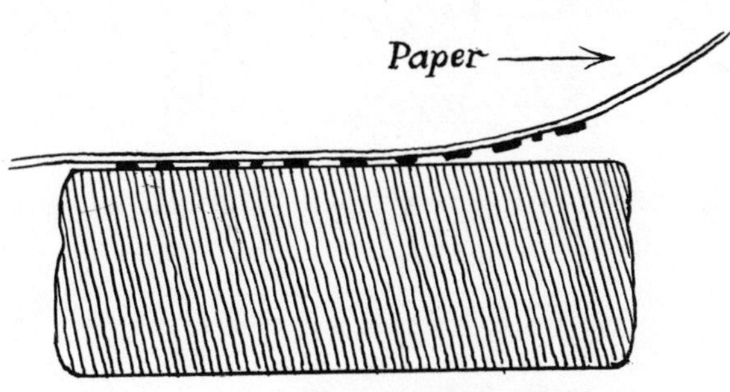

The three basic printing processes

A 15th-century copper engraving by Martin Schongauer

esses. It originated before the middle of the fifteenth century, just about the time Gutenberg started to experiment with letterpress printing and also in the same general region, somewhere along the banks of the river Rhine.

Copper engravings have a beautiful clear and crisp line, the result of the cutting with a sharp steel engraving tool into the copperplate. In inking the plate, the ink is deposited not only in the grooves where it is supposed to be, but also on the surface of the plate. The copperplate printer therefore must wipe off the surface of the plate in order to get a clean impression. In printing, the paper has to be pressed very firmly against every portion of the plate, in order to get the ink in the grooves deposited on the paper.

This calls for a special printing press, constructed somewhat like an old-fashioned clothes-mangle. High pressure is required, and the long handles help the printer get the proper leverage.

This special inking and printing make it impossible to print copperplates with type in one operation. A separate impression, each on a different press, is required for printing letterpress (type, type ornament, woodcuts) and a copper engraving on to the same sheet of paper. In other words, if type matter and engraving are to appear together on a page, this page must pass through two different printing processes. In spite of these complications the fine details possible in copper engraving and the generally sophisticated and refined character of this process made it a very popular one toward the end of the Renaissance.

Copperplate engraving became the major technique not only for full-page illustration, but also for title pages, for single and double frontispieces, for head and tail pieces, and even for initial letters. Architectural elements came to play an important role in Renaissance and baroque illustration and ornamentation.

In the course of the sixteenth and seventeenth centuries the center of gravity in book printing moved from Italy to France, and from there to the Low Countries. From the initial efforts of great individual scholar-printers such as Aldus Manutius in Venice, Henri Estienne in Paris, Christophe Plantin in Antwerp, and the Elzeviers in Leiden, there arose great dynasties of printing and publishing houses, some of which achieved considerable permanence. As the power of the printing press grew, and as secular and church authorities came to understand its political influence, various methods of control were initiated. Restrictive measures and censorship reached serious proportions. The poet Milton wrote an ardent plea for the preservation of the freedom of the press. His *Areopagitica: a Speech of Mr. Milton for the Liberty of Unlicensed Printing, to the Parliament of England*, published in 1644, contains the following words:[1]

"For books are not absolutely dead things, but do contain a potency of life in them to be as active as that soul was whose

[1] Reprinted here in modernized spelling.

progeny they are; nay, they do preserve as in a vial the purest efficacy and extraction of that living intellect that bred them. I know they are as lively, and as vigorously productive, as those fabulous dragon's teeth; and being sown up and down, may chance to spring up armed men. And yet, on the other hand, unless wariness be used, as good almost kill a man as kill a good book; who kills a man kills a reasonable creature, God's image; but he who destroys a good book, kills reason itself, kills the image of God, as it were, in the eye."

Not all the measures of state and church were restrictive, however. The establishment of great official printing houses, such as the Stamperia Vaticana in Rome and the Imprimerie Royale in Paris, had in many ways a beneficial effect on the standards of bookmaking.

In the seventeenth century these standards were generally low. In this period, which witnessed the birth of some of the greatest masterpieces of world literature—from the pen of Shakespeare, Cervantes, and Molière—books were often printed carelessly on poor paper and from types which did not maintain the high perfection of the Renaissance.

There were, of course, some notable exceptions: two of the four great Polyglot Bibles appeared in this century. Polyglot Bibles contain the Holy Scriptures in a number of different languages, printed in parallel columns, making it possible for the student to trace the meaning of a word or a phrase through the various versions of the Bible. Another positive achievement in seventeenth-century bookmaking was in the field of fine bookbinding. Also, the engraving of maps flourished during the period.

There were the great discoveries of courageous explorers and navigators like Columbus, Vespucci, Vasco da Gama, Magellan, Sir Francis Drake. The discovery of the American continent, the circumnavigation of the Cape of Good Hope on the sea route to East India, and many other daring feats of navigation made it possible for the first time in history to trace on maps a reasonably accurate picture of the great land and sea masses that cover the surface of our globe. In the sixteenth century, Italian map makers and, in the seventeenth, dynasties of Dutch map makers and atlas printers supplied the needs of the captains of the Portuguese, Spanish, Dutch, French, and English sailing vessels that conquered the vast sea lanes and laid the foundations of the great colonial empires of the European powers. With them, and often in the immediate wake of the earliest pioneers, came the printers.

The seventeenth century was therefore a time of great expansion in printing. As it was at the time of the invention of printing in Asia and, again, in Europe, so now the fulfillment of the need for religious works came first. In Asia, the demand for the great Buddhist classics, in Europe for the Bible, Missal, and Psalter had created opportunities which were recognized by the earliest printers. When the first printing press in the Western hemisphere had been set up in Mexico City by Juan Pablos in 1539, his first books, too, were religious works.

And now in the seventeenth century, when the first English-American press was set up in Cambridge, Massachusetts, late in 1638, religious books again came first.

The recent founding of a college in Massachusetts, as well as plans for the conversion of the Indians, were foremost in the mind of the Reverend Jose Glover when he purchased a printing press in England and brought it over to Massachusetts. With the press came Stephen Daye, who became the first printer of the colonies. The earliest book to have survived from the output of this press is the famous *Bay Psalm Book*, completed in 1640. Twenty-three years later, in 1663, there appeared John Eliot's translation of the whole of the Bible into the Indian tongue, a triumph over the most difficult circumstances and an eloquent testimony to New England missionary zeal.

Among the many printers in Colonial America at least two names deserve to be mentioned here. One is that of Isaiah Thomas of Worcester, Massachusetts. He was the first man to print on American soil a folio Bible —a Bible of large format—which he completed in 1791. He had a share in both the making of history and the recording of it. As a young man he joined with fervent enthusiasm in the fight for independence. In his more advanced years he strongly felt the need for preserving materials that were part of the history of the new-born American republic. He became the founder and first president of the American Antiquarian Society in Worcester, which today still actively carries out the aims of its founder. Thomas also wrote the first *History of Printing in America* (1810).

The other printer was a man whose fame spread all over the world and whose name is familiar to every school child, not only in America, but also in many other countries of the world: Benjamin Franklin. His career is typical of that of many printers in America in that their chosen profession of printing became for them a stepping stone on the road to political power and distinguished service to their country. However, none of these men quite equaled the record of Benjamin Franklin. He started printing at the age of twelve, went to Philadelphia, alone, unknown, and practically without means as a youth of eighteen. Four years later he owned his own printing plant. He was also in the type, paper, and printing ink business, an importer and dealer in books, and editor of the famous *Poor Richard's Almanac*. His work in the sciences, especially in the field of electricity, was recognized as a contribution of fundamental importance. (I remember how my teacher, forty years ago in Germany, introduced us to "Benjamin Franklin, the inventor of lightning," meaning, of course, the inventor of the lightning conductor.) In 1753 Franklin became Postmaster General of all the British colonies in North America. He was one of the signers of the Declaration of Independence and, at the age of seventy, he went to Paris as the diplomatic representative of his country, successfully exerting his influence to aid the cause of the new-born United States abroad. Most of the educational and scientific institutions and libraries which he founded are still flourishing in Philadelphia, where even today one can feel everywhere the presence of his farsighted and powerfully generous spirit.

The books printed in Colonial America resembled those printed in England, Scotland, and Ireland. In the British Isles the eighteenth century was a period of great progress in bookmaking. For the first time in four hundred years the graphic arts equalled or surpassed standards in continental Europe. The type faces of William Caslon and John Baskerville lent fresh strength and beauty to printed pages. Great strides were made in papermaking, binding, and illustration. Thomas Bewick's new techniques of wood engraving restored to the

Wood engraving by Thomas Bewick for *Aesop's Fables*, 1818

Two Lines Great Primer.

Quouſque tandem
abutere Catilina, p
Quouſque tandem a-
butere, Catilina, pa-

Two Lines Engliſh.

Quouſque tandem abu-
tere, Catilina, patientia
noſtra? quamdiu nos e-
Quouſque tandem abutere
Catilina, patientia noſtra?

Two Lines Pica.

Quouſque tandem abutere,
Catilina, patientia noſtra? qu
Quouſque tandem abutere, Ca-
tilina, patientia noſtra? quam-

William Caslon's roman and italic, in three sizes

Double Pica Roman.

TANDEM aliquando, Quirites! L. Catilinam furentem audacia, ſcelus anhelantem, pe-
A B C D E F G H I J K L M N.

Great Primer Roman.

TANDEM aliquando, Quirites! L. Catilinam furentem audacia, ſcelus anhelantem, peſtem patriæ nefarie molientem, vobis atque huic urbi ferrum flam-
A B C D E F G H I J K L M N O P.

Double Pica Italic.

TANDEM aliquando, Quirites! L. Catilinam furentem audacia, ſcelus anhelantem, peſtem patriæ neſarie moli-
A B C D E F G H I J K L M N.

Great Primer Italic.

TANDEM aliquando, Quirites! L. Catilinam furentem audacia, ſcelus anhelantem, peſtem patriæ neſarie molientem, vobis atque huic urbi ferrum flammamque minitan-
A B C D E F G H I J K L M N O P Q R.

John Baskerville's roman and italic, in two sizes

half-forgotten art of the woodcut a vitality which it has retained to the present day.

In continental Europe, too, the century of enlightenment saw important reforms in printing and bookmaking on the eve of the all-important Industrial Revolution. New techniques of intaglio engraving appeared; color printing came into its own; French engraved books by such artists as Boucher, Fragonard, and Gravelot became a brilliant mirror of an aristocratic society soon to meet its doom; also in France great dynasties of bookbinders created some exquisite masterpieces; in France, too, the families of the Fourniers and the Didots contributed significantly to the esthetic and technical foundations of modern type design and typography. The Italian master Giambattista Bodoni, in Parma, gave to the new classical types their final brilliance and a flexibility which made possible the eventual growth of modern commercial typography (see illus. p. 113).

Here is another good example of the way the spirit of an age is reflected directly and clearly in the design of the books of the period. It is a period which is often called the age of reason, when many outmoded traditions and beliefs were swept aside and when clear thinking and common sense were applied to many scientific and technical problems. The printed page of the eighteenth century shows this new striving for clarity and simple dignity. When looking at the books of this period, you can notice how the words are set apart from each other

MANUALE

TIPOGRAFICO

DEL CAVALIERE

GIAMBATTISTA BODONI

VOLUME PRIMO.

PARMA

PRESSO LA VEDOVA

MDCCCXVIII.

Title page for Giambattista Bodoni's *Manuale Tipografico*, 1818

with extra space between them and how the lines, too, are set wide apart from each other, so as to create a feeling of spaciousness and graceful ease. (The space between lines is called "leading" and, within certain limitations, this space can be as large or as small as the designer of the book wants it to be.)

The eighteenth century also saw the rise of the modern publishing trade. Up to this time many an author had to look to some patron among the aristocracy or high clergy to whom he could dedicate his book in the hope of receiving in return some kind of compensation for his labors. Such a payment was sometimes the only financial reward; at other times it was a much-needed additional income to what his printers were able or willing to pay him. Samuel Johnson, the editor of the famous *Dictionary of the English Language*, broke with the time-honored custom. The prospectus of the *Dictionary* was addressed to the Earl of Chesterfield as the prospective patron. But the few guineas which the great scholar received from the Earl and his social rejection of the author so annoyed Johnson that he broke their relationship in a very dignified and firm letter. The dictionary appeared without dedication to a patron.

Another way of insuring support for a forthcoming work before the time of its publication was the subscription method. Not one, but a group of patrons would agree to purchase the book, and their names would appear in a list of subscribers at the beginning of the volume. Publication by subscription continued through the nineteenth century and in various forms it is still practiced today. However, the eighteenth century witnessed the appearance of the publisher in the modern sense of the word. We now see an individual or firm other than the printer investing money in the writing and printing of books for which the reading public at large is sufficiently numerous to make such an investment profitable. With the arrival on the literary scene of the modern novel, the family magazine, and children's books, writing as a profession began to pay a living wage.

Chapter 10

THE BOOK IN THE NINETEENTH CENTURY

One very interesting thing about the art of printing is the curious way in which tradition and revolution seem to govern its growth. Both the desire for change and a tendency to resist change can be noticed. Many great printers have been very progressive in their technical methods and at the same time very conservative in taste.

We have already seen how the greatest of all revolutions in bookmaking, the invention of printing with movable type, did not do much at first to change the appearance of books. A late medieval manuscript and an early printed book look very much alike.

The same thing was true during the beginnings of the Industrial Revolution, which changed the ancient and noble art of printing into a modern industry.

The tendency of so many printers to avoid radical changes of design is something very interesting to observe. A very good way of doing this is to take one particular feature of the book and see what has hap-

Honor lahor e gloria de nostre senyor deu Jesu christ e dela gloriosa sacratissima verge Maria mare sua senyora nostra, comença la letra del present libre appellat Tirant lo blanch: dirigida per mossen Joanot martorell caualler al serenissimo princep don Ferrando de portogal.

The evolution of the chapter heading

pened to it through several centuries. The opening page of a book, the one on which the text begins, is a clear example. On these pages you will find six different opening pages, selected from books of the fifteenth to the eighteenth century. The first example, No. 1, and the last, No. 6, do not look much alike. Nevertheless they are related to each other in a series of logical steps which form the connecting links. The first example is the opening page of a fifteenth-century manuscript, when title pages had not yet come into use. No. 2 shows how an early printer of the same century cut a border and an initial letter in wood and set his type in such a way as to follow the pattern of the manuscript. Presently, the printer built up border and type from five different blocks, as you can see in No. 3. We are now in the sixteenth century, when title pages had come into use, to show the reader quickly what the book contained,

Prediche utilissime per la quadragesima del reuerẽdo padre frate hieronymo Sauonarola da Ferrara de lordine de frati predicatori sopra Ezechiel propheta: & etiam sopra lo sacro Euangelio.

Aperientur labia mea ut recte predicent. Iusti sunt sermones mei nõ est in eis prauitas neq; quid peruersum. Recti sunt intelligentibus & equi inuenientibus scientiam. Prouerbi. viii.

ΑΠΠΙΑΝΟΥ ΑΛΕΞΑΝΔΡΕΩΣ ΡΩΜΑΙ-ΚΩΝ ΚΕΛΤΙΚΗ.

171. *Page of Grec du Roi: Estienne, Paris,* 1551 (*reduced*)

THE FELICITIES OF SIXTY

IN MY SIXTIETH YEAR, a wise woman of more than eighty said to me: "I congratulate you: you have begun to live after sixty years of preparation, and are now wise enough to govern yourself and help others. The best part of life is between sixty and eighty."

I pondered her saying, testing its truth by my own experience. I think she was right. I think so because my opinion of friends and enemies, of life and the meaning of life, has undergone a marked and significant change in which I find a distinct and abiding happiness. We have. at

CHAPTER I

CAXTON AND HIS LITERARY HERITAGE

The profession of letters has always been a precarious one, and before the advent of printing the lot of the writer was even more unenviable than it was to become in subsequent centuries. We are so accustomed to the highly organized arrangements which exist nowadays in order to bring a writer's wares before the widest, possible public that we are apt to forget how comparatively modern they are, and that the medieval author had little or no means of foreseeing what demand there would be for his work. An impenetrable fog of ignorance or, at best, of, uncertainty left him without knowledge of the work of others. For example, during the fifteenth century, three separate translations were made of the travels of Sir John Mandeville, two of the translators not knowing that the work had already been done. Many other instances might be given to illustrate this difficulty, and on the whole writers were wise to go ahead, oblivious of the labours of others, for the circulation of medieval manuscripts was a fortuitous and patchy affair looked at from a modern point of view.

This patchiness was largely the result of dialect differences in various parts of the country, which made the reading of a work by a London author a matter of difficulty for a reader north of the Trent. Chaucer speaks of the 'gret diversite In Englissh and in writyng of oure tonge', while nearly a century later Caxton is vexed by the same difficulty, and after much thought and research decides that the best he can do is to use 'Englysshe not ouer rude, ne curyous, but in suche termes as shall be understanden by goddyes grace'. Most authors, therefore, found their circulation limited by peculiarities of dialect, and even more perhaps by the uncertain and wellnigh unpre-

The evolution of the chapter heading

the name of the printer, and the address where more copies could be bought. Since the title page was now so important and preceded the opening page, the printer of No. 4 (and of many similar books) felt that he could leave off all but the top bar of the border. Soon the character of its design changed, and in No. 5 we see typographic ornament in place of the traditional woodcut. Eventually, the ornament was left off altogether, as

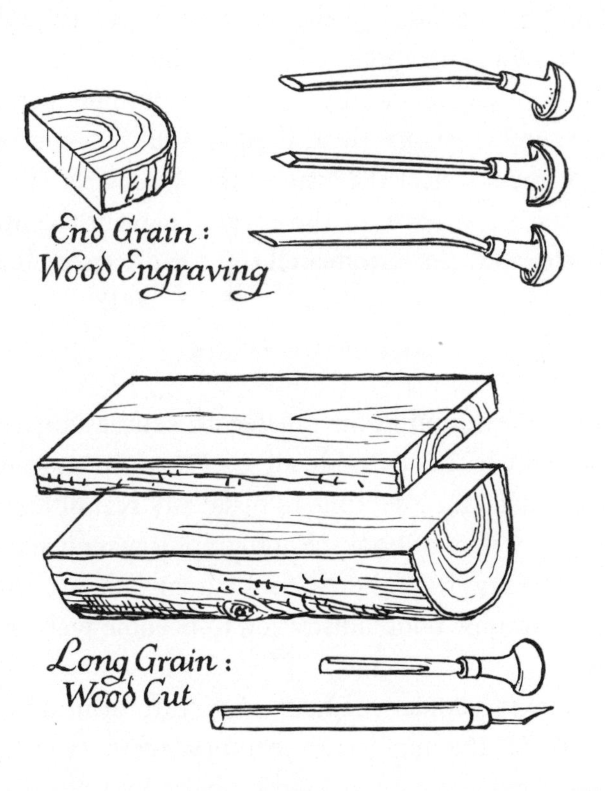

The difference between woodcut and wood engraving

in No. 6, and in many other books since the eighteenth century. All that is left now is some white space. "Sinkage" is what the modern designer calls it. Thus it is literally true to say that chapter headings in many modern books have extra white space above them because the medieval manuscript had no title page! You see then how strong the power of tradition still is in printing.

This has remained true in spite of the tremendous technical developments of the last century and a half.

The books printed in the nineteenth century, when all these new inventions were tried out, do not look especially "machine made." There is nothing particularly technical about their design. On the contrary, many of them reflect the taste of the "romantic" school of writing so popular in the early nineteenth century or, a little later, the sentimentality of the Victorian age.

BOOK ILLUSTRATION

Book illustration in the nineteenth century furnishes an especially good example of the way inventions in graphic arts take a long time to make any real difference in the appearance of books. Photography was an accomplished fact by 1839, but it took about half a century for photographic book illustration to become well established.

The most popular methods of picture printing during most of the nineteenth century were two hand processes: wood engraving and lithography.

Wood engraving, the invention of Thomas Bewick of Newcastle, is a relief process, like the woodcut. But it has much more delicate lines, and much finer details can be cut into the block. A very skilled wood engraver can follow the lines of a pen drawing almost exactly. The technical reason for the fine lines lies in the use of a very hard wood, namely boxwood (which is cut into blocks against the grain, instead of with the grain as in the woodcut). The surface of the boxwood block is so hard and smooth that special engraving tools, like the ones the engraver uses on copper or steel plates, are necessary.

The other new process, lithography, was invented in Munich by Aloys Senefelder, who lived from 1771 to 1834. This process, the earliest example of planographic printing, already mentioned on page 100, is altogether different from any printing method we have discussed so far. It is a surface process, in which the printing ink is not deposited on the raised parts of the plate, or sunk into grooves. Instead, it is placed flat on the surface.

In lithography, the proper distribution of the ink on the printing surface is governed by a simple fact of nature, namely that water and oil do not mix. (Why does water "run off a duck's back"? Because the duck has a gland that secretes a certain kind of grease which it distributes with its beak all over its coat of feathers before diving.) In lithography, or "stone writing," the artist makes a drawing with ink or crayon directly onto

„Er war Ihr Geliebter, Madame!“ (Bravo! bravo!)
„Ich mußte ihn töten!“ (Bravo! bravo!)
„Ich habe ihn getötet!“ (Bravo! bravo!)
„Ich werde auch Sie töten!“ (Bravo! bravo!)

A lithograph by Honoré Daumier

the surface of a special type of polished stone, using an ink or crayon with a high grease content. After the stone is lightly etched, water is applied to its surface, to fix the image on the stone. The water covers all parts of the surface except the places where there is the greasy writing or drawing. Next, lithographic printing ink, which has a high grease content, is rolled onto the stone. This printing ink joins the ink left from the original drawing, but is rejected by the watery surface of the stone everywhere else. An impression can now be pulled in a lithographic press. For each new impression water is again applied, and then the stone is re-inked.

The new process at once proved its usefulness in many directions. It was employed in music printing, map making, in early commercial printing, for political and social caricatures in the new monthly and weekly magazines, and in numerous other ways. Its chief use in nineteenth-century bookmaking was for decoration and for various kinds of illustration. The soft tones of a lithograph invited hand coloring, which was often used with charming effect. Eventually the lithographs were printed in several colors.

THE RISE OF CHILDREN'S BOOKS

One of the fields of illustration which benefited especially from the many ways of picture printing was the children's picture book. This was one of the new kinds of books which, after some early experiments in the eighteenth century, really blossomed forth in the nineteenth century.

Children have always enjoyed looking at picture books, and it is certain that through the ages they must have been keenly interested in many of the illustrated books which they had a chance to see in the hands of adults. But with very few exceptions those were books not intended especially for youngsters. It is difficult to imagine that a little more than a century and a half ago there was hardly such a thing as a picture book made for the enjoyment of children. Primers and other kinds of readers and schoolbooks would of course have some pictures in them, but they were used strictly as teaching aids or as a means of demonstrating the proper behavior of a young person. Well into the nineteenth century do we find this element of moral instruction mixed in with attempts to give children amusing and enjoyable pictures. John Newbery of London was one of the first publishers in the English-speaking world to make genuine picture books for children. He published a *Mother Goose* as early as about 1760. The Newbery Medal, which is awarded each year to an illustrated children's book of outstanding merit, is named after him.

Some of the most famous children's books of all ages owe their birth to amateurs. *Slovenly Peter* (or *Struwelpeter*, as it was called in the original German) started out as a collection of drawings and simple verses which Heinrich Hoffmann, a friendly doctor of Frankfurt, made during his visits to sick children, to calm them down if they were afraid of him, and to amuse them. It was first published in 1847.

Alice in Wonderland, as some of you may know, was a story first told by an Oxford lecturer of mathematics to three young girls on a pleasant summer afternoon spent rowing on the river. Lewis Carroll later wrote the story down in a book for Alice, his favorite, as a Christmas present and illustrated it with amateurish and very charming drawings. When the book appeared in print in 1865, Sir John Tenniel based his pictures on these ingenious and funny amateur drawings.

Perhaps you are wondering why it took so long for genuine children's books to become available. After all, the art of printing was about three centuries old when they first appeared in the eighteenth century. It is difficult to explain this delay in a few words, and many different factors have to be taken into consideration. In a general way we can say that the great social changes of the eighteenth century were responsible for the birth of the children's book. The new understanding of the position of man as a free individual rather than as the servant of Church, State, or Monarch, the ideas and conditions which brought forth the Bill of Rights, new ideals in education, the concept of free development and growth, all these things combined to make possible books intended for children.

Another new kind of book which made its first appearance in the nineteenth century was the comic book. The art of telling a story in a string of closely connected pictures is practically as old as, or perhaps older than, the art of writing. Medieval illumination and early printing made excellent use of what we might call "animated" technique. Popular broadsides, plain and colored, continued the tradition into the early nineteenth century.

The Geneva artist, Rodolphe Töpffer, was the first man to use the easy flow of the pen and ink on the lithographic stone for a series of amusing satirical picture books. He even dreamed up the soundtrack, a zigzag line, which he drew under his pictures at a time when the scientists were only just beginning to experiment with sound recording. Gustave Doré, one of the most popular French illustrators of the last century, made his first comic book while a schoolboy of fifteen. This happened in 1847, and we must not forget that the ingenious young draftsman knew the secret of dissected motion (the use of a series of closely related pictures, each showing a more advanced stage of an action), many years before the motion picture camera came into existence. After him came Wilhelm Busch, the great German master of the nineteenth-century comic book. His picture book of the two naughty boys, *Max and Moritz*, has been fascinating children ever since its first appearance in 1865 (the same year *Alice in Wonderland* was first printed). *Max and Moritz* had a great deal to do with the rise of the American comic strip. The "Katzenjammer Kids" were developed by

Max and Moritz

Rudolph Dirks for the New York *Journal* in the year 1897 along the lines of the Munich picture book. H. H. Knorr continued this strip when Dirks left the *Journal* in 1914 and started a similar cartoon, "The Captain and the Kids," for the New York *World*.

BOOKMAKING BECOMES AN INDUSTRY

By the end of the century, the old manual processes of printing had been replaced by mechanical production with power-driven machinery. The mechanization of one process, in order to be truly effective, necessitated the industrialization of all other processes. The introduction of power and of fast-rotating cylinders heightened the pressure for the elimination of production bottlenecks resulting from still surviving manual processes. What was the use of stepping up production of paper from an output of hundreds or even a few thousand separate sheets of handmade paper a day to more than sixty feet of paper a minute on machines producing continuous rolls, if type could not be set fast enough to use up these vast new quantities? Or, what was the advantage of printing thousands of sheets of paper an hour on a power press instead of a few hundred on the old hand press, if you still had to bind them into books by hand? Bookbinding, which had been done by hand for about 1,500 years, now had to be completely mechanized. The casing-in process and the use of cloth as a cover material, starting early in the nineteenth century, made this possible.

The main difference between the old and the new method is briefly this: In traditional hand binding the printed sheets are folded into signatures (units of four, eight, sixteen, or even thirty-two pages each, depending on whether the sheet is folded twice, three times, or four or five times) and then sewn to cords or bands which are laced into or pasted onto covers of wood or cardboard; these are then covered with parchment, leather, or paper and decorated and lettered. In machine binding, the case (or cover), which is usually cloth over cardboard, is made as a separate unit and stamped with lettering and decoration before it is attached to the book. Casing-in is the attaching of this cover to the sewn book; it is done by pasting a hinge of cloth around the back of the book and to the insides of the front and back cover; the hinge is covered by the endpapers, which are the pages (often decorated with a map or other illustration and usually made of heavier paper than the rest of the book) pasted in at the beginning and the end of the volume.

The old wooden, and the more recent iron hand presses gave way to power-driven cylinder presses, the first practical operation having been started in 1812 in London by Friedrich Koenig. Later, in New York City, Richard Hoe's "Type Revolving Machine" first solved the problem of mounting type on a cylinder, but the introduction of stereotyping offered a more practical solution. In stereotyping, impressions are made not directly from type onto paper, but into pliable papier-

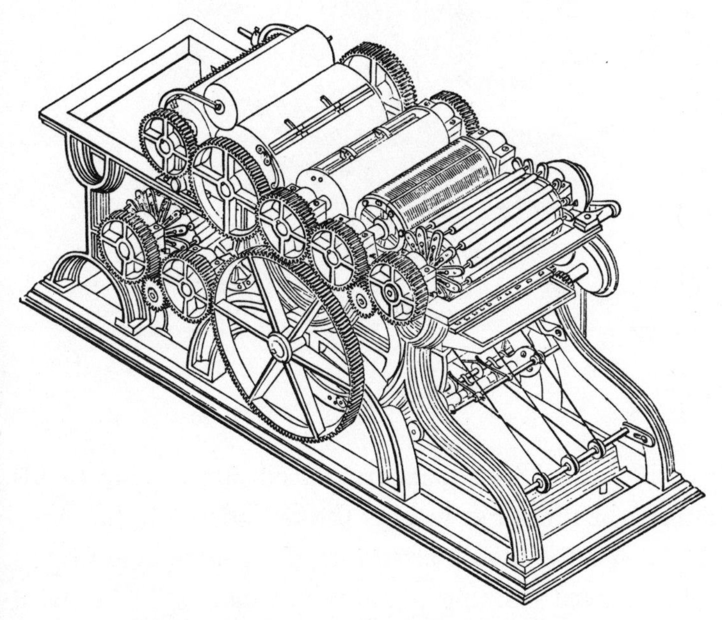

Bullock's Patent Rotary Perfecting Press

The Linotype

mâché mats. These mats are placed into casting molds curved in the same way as the cylinders of the press. Type metal is then poured into these mats, resulting in solid, curved printing plates which can easily be fitted onto the cylinder of the press. This method is used daily in newspaper printing and can be observed on a visit to a newspaper plant.

Printing from solid plates instead of directly from type is practiced not only in newspaper and magazine production, but also for books. When mass production came into book printing, it was soon discovered that type would wear out too quickly in the rapid printing of large editions. Plates which are made from type by means of electrotyping and in recent years also from plastics, wear better, are easier to handle in mass production, and are also more easily stored away for future reprinting.

The setting of type by machine, the most complicated problem of all, was solved, after innumerable trials and errors, by Ottmar Mergenthaler's Linotype (see p. 130), by the Intertype, by Tolbert Lanston's Monotype (see p. 132), and other composing machines. It is important to understand that these machines have not completely replaced hand composition. For certain typographic problems, such as title pages and chapter headings in books, and for a good deal of commercial display composition, typesetting by hand is still used. Type set by hand today is called foundry type.

In the field of illustration, Daguerre's invention of photography in 1839 was soon applied to all processes of pictorial reproduction: line engraving and halftone engraving in relief printing; photogravure and rotogravure in intaglio; and photolithography, offset, and collotype in planographic printing.

The processes all have this in common: the picture to be printed is no longer cut into or drawn onto the plate, but photographed onto it. It is then treated with chemi-

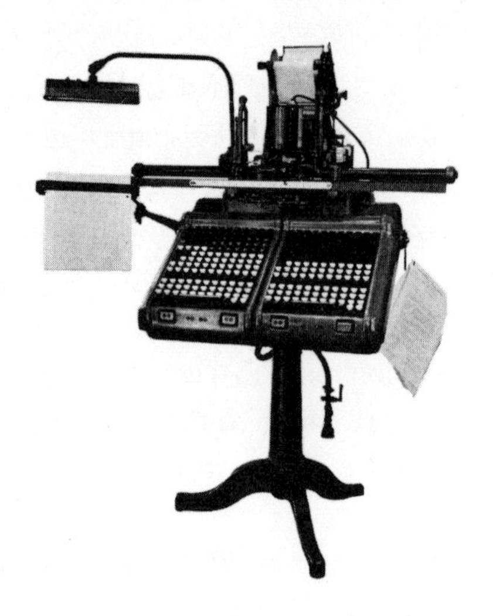

The Monotype: keyboard (above) and caster (below)

cals in such a way that when the rollers pass over the plate, the ink is deposited only where it is needed in order to reproduce the image. Depending on the process, the lines and dots of the picture are made to stand out (relief), or etched into (intaglio), or fixed on the surface (planographic) of the plate.[1]

American inventors and engineers took an early interest in the graphic arts revolution, but in the first part of the nineteenth century it was in England and on the continent that the important inventions were first tried out. By mid-century, in the years before the Civil War, the United States had caught up and was beginning to make some outstanding contributions of its own which other countries started to follow. By the end of the century, American leadership in industrial development was clearly established. Some of the most important graphic arts processes, such as the Linotype and the Monotype composing machines, now used all over the world, are American contributions.

[1] If you would like to know more about photomechanical printing, consult the Bibliography on page 227.

Chapter 11

THE REVOLT AGAINST THE MACHINE

Some years ago, when I was on a vacation in Austria, it became necessary for me to see a dentist. The man recommended by my friends turned out to be a most distinguished old scientist, the director of the university's dental clinic. When I sat in his chair and watched him prepare for the treatment, I was struck with terror. His drill was a kind I had never seen before, a very primitive old-fashioned instrument which did not use electric current but had to be operated by a foot-pedal. Thoughts of medieval torture crowded my mind. Great was my surprise and relief when it turned out that the old gentleman handled the instrument with the utmost tenderness and delicacy. His foot and hand controlled the drill perfectly and never before had a treatment been so painless and easy.

This experience taught me the great lesson that a power-driven machine is not necessarily superior to a tool in the hands of a skilled craftsman. The machine

W. A. DWIGGINS ~~30 Ipswich Street~~ BOSTON

Hingham Center Mass.

Dear Mr. Lehmann-Haupt:

Here is the second communication for your portfolio. The ink that I use is Higgins Eternal Writing Ink in a comfortable Moore fountain-pen; and my filing system is much more primitive than any used by the earlier Mesopotamian civilizations. Your comments make me self-conscious, of course, and spoil the fine free sweep that characterizes my usual hand-writing. . . . .

Your article for ZS für BF was held over, no doubt, until the temperature of publication would climb up to the 102° when you wrote it, so August is very likely. I should like to see it, because I perceive that you are one of those who can penetrate to the core of the Püterschein Affair and state the cold facts — even at 102°

Sincerely

W. A. Dwiggins

May 27 1934

An example of calligraphy, by the late William A. Dwiggins

can save time and labor, speed up transportation and communication, penetrate into the outer space and split the atom; it can store up and reproduce sounds and images. But it can do these things only as an instrument in the hands of man, as his servant. Wherever the machine becomes mightier than the human being, whenever and wherever it happens that man loses control over the machine, there is great danger. This is true not only of machines which destroy lives and property. The souls and minds of human beings too can become unduly dominated by machines. Machines in themselves are neither good nor bad. It is the use we make of them which counts.

The world of printing shows us these things very clearly. The majority of books printed in the world today are machine-made. Their type is set mechanically, the pictures are produced photomechanically, the impression is performed by rapidly moving power presses on machine-made paper, and the volumes are bound by machines. Yet, strangely enough, in many countries there are men and women today who still practice the graphic arts in the time-honored way of centuries ago. Like the monks in the medieval monasteries, people in the twentieth century still practice calligraphy, the art of beautiful writing. There are bookbinders today who can bind books by hand in costly leather and parchment. The arts of woodcutting and wood engraving, of copper engraving, etching, and lithography, once threatened with extinction, have spread again all over the world.

They are taught in thousands of schools and colleges. The highly skilled craft of papermaking by hand is practiced in many countries of Europe and Asia, and beautiful sheets of white, colored, and decorated papers can be bought in the United States.

It is true that these crafts are old ones, practiced for many centuries. This does not mean, however, that the work turned out today by the men and women engaged in these ancient crafts is old-fashioned in character and backward in taste. On the contrary, some very fresh and surprisingly modern works of art have been produced by these old hand methods. Very often they offer more freedom to the artist, more opportunity for imaginative creation, than the most modern mechanical processes. Photography, to give one example, is a wonderful invention which has had a most profound influence on the graphic arts. Many interesting and beautiful photographs are produced every year which are worthy of being hung on the walls of our museums and homes and which make fitting illustrations for many kinds of books. But photographs are neither the only, nor always the most accurate way of describing objects, or of depicting the beauties of nature. There are artists today who can do these things by drawing pictures, cutting woodcuts, making lithographs or etchings which are often at least as effective as photographs. When it comes to illustrating a story or expressing feelings or emotions in pictures, photographs are very rarely as successful as the older picture-printing methods.

It is surprising to realize how many of the ancient skills have survived in the machine age and how many people are once again practicing them. How has this come about?

A little more than half a century ago, at just about the time when the industrialization of the graphic arts was completed, a few farsighted people grew uneasy about the future of the ancient and noble art of printing.

In Victorian England, the poet and social reformer, William Morris, spoke out strongly against the loss of beauty and dignity in printing:

". . . a book, printed or written, has a tendency to be a beautiful object, and that we of this age should generally produce ugly books, shows, I fear, something like malice pretense —a *determination* to put our eyes in our pockets whenever we can . . ."[1]

". . . I began printing books," he explained, "with the hope of producing some which would have a definite claim to beauty, while at the same time they should be easy to read . . ."[2]

William Morris went back to the beginnings of printing. He obtained the services of a paper mill which still remembered how to make good strong rag paper by the old hand method. With the help of Emery Walker (who later became Sir Emery in recognition of his services to the graphic arts), he created some bold typefaces based on Gothic and on Nicolaus Jenson's Roman type.

[1] In his *The Ideal Book.*

[2] In his *A Note by William Morris on his Aims in founding the Kelmscott Press.*

He designed and cut some beautiful strong initials and borders. He inspired some of his fellow-artists, such as Sir Edward Burne-Jones, Walter Crane, and Dante Gabriel Rossetti, to make woodcuts for his edition of medieval romances and legends, for his Chaucer edition, and for his own writings.

His influence was tremendous. The books printed by William Morris at the Kelmscott Press showed that the dignity of craftsmanship was capable of surviving the impact of industrialization.

This example was followed in many parts of the world. Men of culture and vision established private presses that demonstrated the new beauty and the fresh strength which grew from the revival of the arts and crafts. The example of the Kelmscott Press was followed by such private presses as the Doves Press and the Ashendene Press in England, and the Bremer Presse in Germany. In America, William Morris had a profound effect on Daniel Berkeley Updike in Boston, the founder of the Merrymount Press; on Frederic Goudy, America's most prolific type designer; and on its greatest typographer, Bruce Rogers. Quality printing houses, such as the Curwen Press in England, which produced some of the fine books of the Nonesuch Press, and American printing plants like William Edwin Rudge's and Elmer Adler's applied the arts and crafts ideal to a wider field. In France, the traditional collaboration between great artists and skilled printers continued into the twentieth century. Such famous artists as Manet,

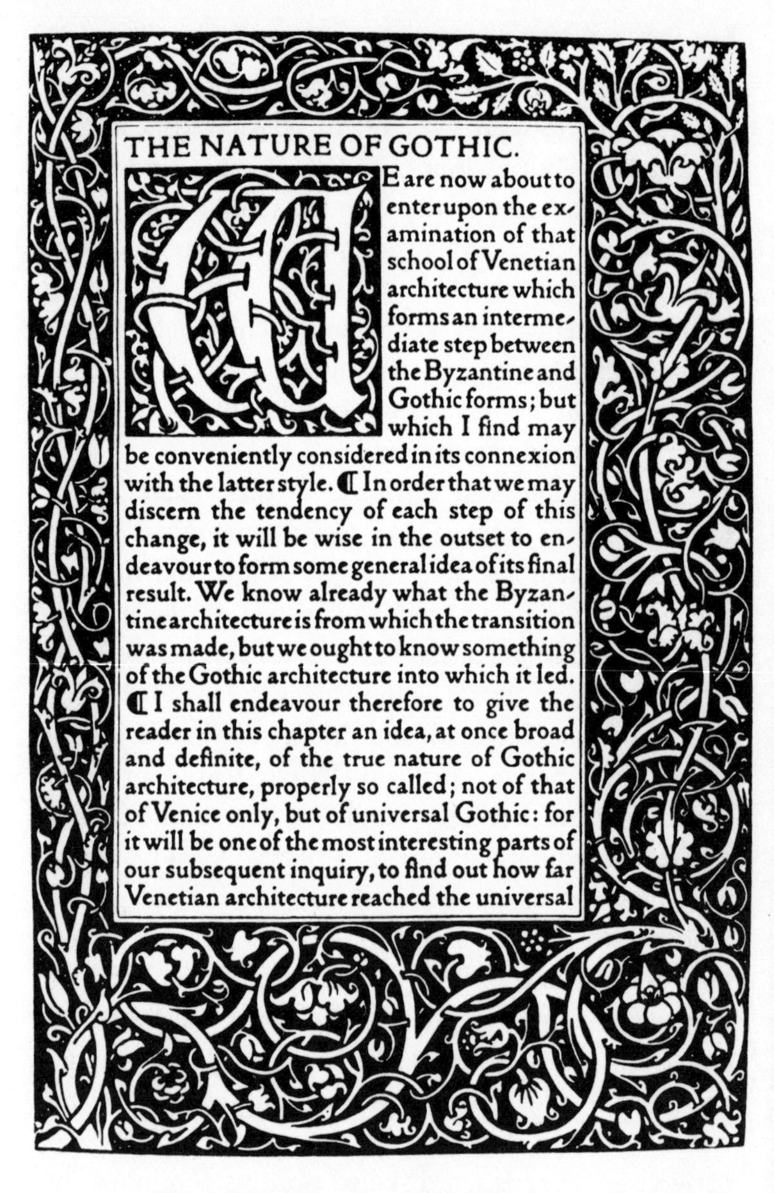

THE NATURE OF GOTHIC.

WE are now about to enter upon the examination of that school of Venetian architecture which forms an intermediate step between the Byzantine and Gothic forms; but which I find may be conveniently considered in its connexion with the latter style. ¶ In order that we may discern the tendency of each step of this change, it will be wise in the outset to endeavour to form some general idea of its final result. We know already what the Byzantine architecture is from which the transition was made, but we ought to know something of the Gothic architecture into which it led. ¶ I shall endeavour therefore to give the reader in this chapter an idea, at once broad and definite, of the true nature of Gothic architecture, properly so called; not of that of Venice only, but of universal Gothic: for it will be one of the most interesting parts of our subsequent inquiry, to find out how far Venetian architecture reached the universal

A page from John Ruskin's *Nature of Gothic*, printed in 1892 by William Morris

Toulouse-Lautrec, Rodin, Maillol, Matisse, Picasso, Rouault, and others made magnificent book illustrations.

Early in the twentieth century, the revival of the arts and crafts spread also to the production of regular trade books in Europe. In the United States the same thing happened in the twenties, stimulated by the efforts of William Addison Dwiggins, the highly gifted calligrapher, type designer, and illustrator, and by the encouragement of the American Institute of Graphic

Woodcut by Aristide Maillol

Arts. Textbooks, children's books, and other kinds of special books have begun to show the beneficial effect of the rediscovery of the ancient belief that beauty and utility can go together. Wonderful results are possible when this belief is shared by the publisher and his book designer.

THE BOOK DESIGNER—MASTER OF THE MACHINE

Book designing is a new profession, the result of specialization. In the days of early printing one man, sometimes aided by only a few assistants, would perform in his own workshop all the tasks necessary to turn a manuscript into a printed book. The separation of his activities into distinct skills, trades, and professions came about very gradually. In the eighteenth century, around the time when American colonists began to fight for their independence from the English Crown, the present division of trades and professions in printing and bookselling became recognizable.

This was true more in Europe than in America. For here, along the eastern seaboard, when printing was first practiced in the English-speaking colonies, something very interesting took place. The early American printer, like his ancestor in fifteenth-century Europe, once again had to become a jack-of-all-trades. In *The Book in America*, Lawrence C. Wroth, one of the greatest experts on Colonial printing, has pointed out that the printing shop of the Colonial small town became from its very nature a center of community life. It was the clearing house for local information as well as for news from the outside world. Frequently, the printer was also the postmaster of his town, so that in the course of a day many people came to his shop. On his shelves, therefore, were to be found all sorts of assorted merchandise, including cough medicine, sealing wax, chocolate, lemons, writing paper, pens, and fiddle strings. It was only natural that his own books and, often, books from other publishers in both England and America were part of his stock. The progressive printer regarded his importation and sale of books as a service to the community almost as important as his printing.

The variety of merchandise still to be found today in many American bookshops is perhaps a kind of survival from those days. However, the printing business has become strictly separated from retail selling, and it is actually a highly specialized industry today with many firms operating only as composing houses, or only as printers of certain types of pictures, and so on.

How is a book manufactured today?

THE MANUFACTURING PROCESS

Let us remember that we started out, at the beginning of this book, to trace a volume through its various stages of production from the desk of the author to the finished product in the hands of the reader. Things are managed very differently today from the time when one man could produce in his own workshop as many copies of a book as he needed for an edition. In mid-twentieth century, the services of a number of different, separate organizations and services are required: they have to be planned for and fitted together very carefully. When a publisher has accepted a book for publication and after his editorial department has prepared the manuscript for production, it is turned over to the manufacturing department. Here, the following steps are taken:

After the format of the book has been planned by the book designer, the manuscript is sent to a printing firm or composition house. Then the illustrations have to be provided for. The author may already have furnished all the pictures necessary for the book. Otherwise, a professional illustrator must be called in to make the pictures. Plates for the illustrations are now ordered at a photoengraving plant, or at a similar specialized establishment, depending on the process of reproduction that has been chosen for the pictures. Sometimes more than one method is needed, as for instance, when a book has diagrams and also drawings in the text (which can be reproduced by one of several "line" processes), and also full-page plates such as photographs in black and white or in color (which require the use of a "halftone" process).[1] The plates have to be ready and in the hands

[1] The book you are now reading has been printed by the offset process. The type matter, Fritz Kredel's drawings, the reproductions and examples in line, as well as those in halftone, like the one on page 130, have all been assembled into their proper positions on the pages of the book by pasting type and pictures together. The pages were then photographed on zinc plates and printed 32 at a time.

of the printer when he is ready to "go to press." Paper for the book has to be ordered from a paper mill and arrangements have to be made for it to be on hand when needed. In the meantime, covers for the book are being prepared at a bookbinding plant and scheduled so as to be ready when the printed sheets arrive from the printer. The book jacket must also be ready at this time, so that when the books are bound, the jackets can be wrapped around the covers. Then the finished books can be sent to the warehouse, from which point the orders of booksellers, libraries, and individual readers are filled.

The manufacturing process is not always the same as described here. Many variations are possible from book to book. For instance, printing and binding may be done in the same plant, or one printer may provide the text of a book and another the section containing the pictures. The different plants cooperating in the production of a book are not always located in the same city, and sometimes not even in the same country. After the last war, publishers in America discovered that occasionally it would be worth their while to have certain jobs done in Europe.

It is easy to understand that the various steps in book production have to be planned ahead of time very carefully and coordinated in such a way that they all fit into each other.

The responsibility for this coordination rests with the publisher's manufacturing department, and it is a procedure which requires careful and conscientious handling. But even the most perfect scheduling of the manufacturing process would never result in a really successful job of book production unless there were a master plan behind it all. This is where the book designer comes in. His is the real responsibility for the creation of the book. He performs for the future readers the same service which an architect performs for the future inhabitant of a house which he builds.

The architect makes a plan in which he considers the purpose of the building, the site on which it is to be erected, and the available funds. He selects the materials and the methods of construction. He supervises the actual building, helps solve unforeseen problems, and attends to innumerable details. In all these activities he is guided by the desire not only to erect a serviceable and economical structure but also to create something beautiful. He wants to give his buildings a feeling of grace and ease which will satisfy the eye of the beholder. He hopes to create a building which will not only do credit to his own sense of good taste but will also add dignity and beauty to the place where it is erected. We see many ugly apartment houses and factory buildings, gas stations, and supermarkets grow up in many parts of the country. Their lack of beauty is often due to the absence of an architect. These buildings are put up as cheaply and as quickly as possible, without any pride, without the knowledge that dignity and beauty are not unnecessary luxuries, but are important parts of our lives.

The desire for beauty is a natural and healthy part of the pursuit of happiness. We are not always aware of this, and some people are actually ashamed to admit that they care about such things. Nevertheless, hunger for beauty is an essential part of the heritage of the human race.

What is true of an architect is equally true of a book designer. There is this difference: the architect creates buildings which house human beings and their innumerable activities; the book designer, on the other hand, creates volumes which house words and pictures through which man imparts and obtains information, finds relaxation and entertainment, and expresses his dreams. The book is the tangible, physical abode of the spirit of man.

Like ugly buildings, ugly books are all around us; we also find many printed volumes which are neither good nor bad. Anyone who appreciates good workmanship can recognize very quickly that many books "just happened." They were turned out carelessly and without love, routine products of the manufacturing process. Such volumes came into existence without the helping hand of an experienced designer.

As I write down these words, I can almost hear some people exclaim: "But what does this man want? Surely, he does not expect all books to be beautiful? That is an impossible demand"; to which I reply: "It is not nearly so impossible as you may think. And it is not nearly so expensive as you imagine. Think a moment. No matter how you look at it, paper and cloth have to be bought, the type must be set, the sheets run through the press, and so on. Comparatively little added attention, labor, and very little extra money is needed to plan all these steps in such a way that they really fit together into a harmonious unit, which is what we mean when we speak of beauty in printing. And it is exactly here that the book designer fits into the picture."

How does he perform his task?

The book lies before him in the form of a typewritten manuscript, with or without pictures. The first thing he does is to read the manuscript, or as much of it as is necessary so that he can become acquainted with the contents, can "get the feel" of the book.

Next, he will make a first rough estimate of the length of the manuscript and the number of the plates and other illustrations, if any. He will see if there are any special production problems involved, such as complicated tables or diagrams, maps, musical notes, footnotes, or various kinds of appendices.

He is now ready to visualize in a general way what the book shall be like. He considers by whom and under what circumstances it will be read or consulted and decides whether it should be a thick or thin, light or heavy, tall or small volume. He will seek ways and means of expressing in the appearance of the book something of its character and style. He will decide whether to do this forcefully and by obvious means, or more unobtrusively and indirectly.

In all these decisions he is guided by the desire not to interfere with the message of the book but rather to strengthen its appeal. He thinks of the author of the book and how he can best help him to speak to his public, like the producer of a play who strives to make the words of the playwright come alive on the stage.

ABOUT THE BOOK ILLUSTRATOR

In these efforts the book designer can be aided greatly by the book illustrator. His work, too, bears a resemblance to the task of the producer of a play. The illustrator has to translate the scenery and the characters created by the words of the author into concrete, visual images. He has to draw the people in the book in such a way that they really act out the story. He has to animate the characters, as the animators in the Walt Disney Studio do. But the book illustrator must not steal the show from the author. He must remember that his pictures should supplement the story. His purpose is to help the reader to understand the situation and, perhaps, to recognize the characters, and in a general way to increase his enjoyment of the story.

There are of course exceptions to this rule. Publishers sometimes put out books which are built around a series of pictures as the most important part of their contents. This is so, for instance, in a picture book for small children, or in a volume containing a collection of important photographs, or reproductions of famous paintings. In these cases the text is often very properly nothing more than a guide to the understanding and appreciation of the plates. The book designer is then faced with the special problem of making the many pictures and the few words go well together. There are even whole books which tell a story completely without words, in pictures only.

You can easily find out about these various possibilities by doing a little experimenting on your own. Try to make some pictures for one of your favorite stories. Before you begin, read the story over again and find out which character and situations you would select for illustration. Think about how you would draw these scenes, and then go ahead and make some sketches. It is fun to do this in a group, when several people read the same story and each makes his own pictures. The comparison of the results will be very amusing.

Then, for another experiment, try to tell a story all in pictures, as it is done in a cartoon but, if possible, get along without speech balloons. It is easiest to select a familiar subject, some personal experience perhaps, like a day in the life of your family, a vacation experience, or a holiday celebration. Trying to draw these illustrations or stories yourself will probably be not nearly so difficult as you might have thought. Whatever you may think of the results of your efforts, such an experiment will help you greatly to understand and appreciate the work of professional illustrators. It will also give you a better idea of the task of the book designer, which is what this chapter is really about. It is time for us to return to watch him at work.

HOW THE DESIGN IS WORKED OUT

The first thing the designer will really work out in detail on paper is the text page of the book he is designing. To get a readable and attractive page layout, he must balance a great number of elements against each other. He has to select a suitable typeface and the size in which it is to be set; decide whether the composition should be close and narrow, average or wide (this is called spacing between letters and words); how long the line should be; whether the lines should be close together or have some space between them (this is called leading); how many lines there are to be on a page; and how much margin should surround the text on all four sides. All these decisions have a very important influence on the total appearance of the book. For instance, if the manuscript is short and a big page is chosen, a large, thin volume will result. If the book contains, for instance, intimate little short stories, this would not be the ideal format, and another plan would have to be worked out.

Next, the chapter headings will have to be planned; also the index and appendix, bibliographical section, etc., and the front matter. Contents page and title page especially are very important, because they are read first and should tell the reader as much as necessary about the insides of the book. A good title page can greatly en-

Columbus needs a planet to shape his course upon. Newton and Laplace need myriads of age and thick-strewn celestial areas. One may say a gravitating solar system is already prophesied in the nature of Newton's mind. Not less does the brain of Davy or of Gay-Lussac, from childhood exploring the affinities and repulsions of particles, anticipate the laws of organization. Does not the eye of the human embryo predict the light? the ear of Handel predict the witchcraft of harmonic sound? Do not the constructive fingers of Watt, Fulton, Whittemore, Arkwright, predict the fusible, hard, and temperable texture of metals, the properties of stone, water, and wood? Do not the lovely attributes of the maiden child predict the refinements and decorations of civil society? Here also we are reminded of the action of man on man. A mind might ponder its thoughts for ages and not gain so much self-knowledge as the passion of love shall teach it in a day. Who knows himself before he has been thrilled with indignation at an outrage, or has heard an eloquent tongue, or has shared the throb of thousands in a national exultation or alarm? No man can antedate his experience, or guess what faculty or feeling a new object shall unlock, any more than he can draw to-day the face of a person whom he shall see to-morrow for the first time.

I will not now go behind the general statement to explore the reason of this correspondency. Let it suffice that in the light of these two facts, namely, that the mind is One, and that nature is its correlative, history is to be read and written.

Thus in all ways does the soul concentrate and reproduce its treasures for each pupil. He too shall pass through the whole cycle of experience. He shall collect into a focus the rays of nature. History no longer shall be a dull book. It shall walk incarnate in every just and wise man. You shall not tell me by languages and titles a catalogue of the volumes you have read. You shall make me feel what periods you have lived. A man shall be the Temple of Fame. He shall walk, as the poets have described that goddess, in a robe painted all over with wonderful events and experiences;—his own form and features by their exalted intelligence shall be that variegated vest. I shall find in him the Foreworld; in his childhood the Age of Gold, the Apples of Knowledge, the Argonautic Expedition, the calling of Abraham, the building of the Temple, the Advent of Christ, Dark Ages, the Revival of Letters, the Reformation, the discovery of new lands, the opening of new sciences and new regions in man. He shall be the priest of Pan, and bring with him into humble cottages the blessing of the morning stars, and all the recorded benefits of heaven and earth.

Is there somewhat overweening in this claim? Then I reject all I have written, for what is the use of pretending to know what we know not? But it is the fault of our rhetoric that we cannot strongly state one fact without seeming to belie some other. I hold our actual knowledge very cheap. Hear the rats in the wall, see the lizard on the fence, the fungus under foot, the lichen on the log. What do I know sympathetically, morally, of either of these worlds of life? As old as the Caucasian man,—perhaps older,—these creatures have kept their counsel beside him, and there is no record of any word or sign that has passed from one to the other. What connection do the books show between the fifty or sixty chemical elements and the historical eras? Nay, what does history yet record of the metaphysical annals of

17

1. Lines too wide for the size of type

We are always coming up with the emphatic facts of history in our private experience and verifying them here. All history becomes subjective; in other words there is properly no history, only biography. Every mind must know the whole lesson for itself, — must go over the whole ground. What it does not see, what it does not live, it will not know. What the former age has epitomized into a formula or rule for manipular convenience, it will lose all the good of verifying for itself, by means of the wall of that rule. Somewhere, sometime, it will demand and find compensation for that loss, by doing the work itself. Ferguson discovered many things in astronomy which had long been known. The better for him.

History must be this or it is

19

2. Lines too narrow for the size of type

Virtues are, in the popular estimate, rather the exception than the rule. There is the man *and* his virtues. Men do what is called a good action, as some piece of courage or charity, much as they would pay a fine in expiation of daily non-appearance on parade. Their works are done as an apology or extenuation of their living in the world,—as invalids and the insane pay a high board. Their virtues are penances. I do not wish to expiate, but to live. My life is for itself and not for a spectacle. I much prefer that it should be of a lower strain, so it be genuine and equal, than that it should be glittering and unsteady. I wish it to be sound and sweet, and not to need diet and bleeding. I ask primary evidence that you are a man, and refuse this appeal from the man to his actions. I know that for myself it makes no difference whether I do or forbear those actions which are reckoned excellent. I cannot consent to pay for a privilege where I have intrinsic right. Few and mean as my gifts may be, I actually am, and do not need for my own assurance or the assurance of my fellows any secondary testimony.

What I must do is all that concerns me, not what the people think. This rule, equally arduous in actual and in intellectual life, may serve for the whole distinction between greatness and meanness. It is the harder because you will always find those who think they know what is your duty better than you know it. It is easy in the world to live after the world's opinion; it is easy in solitude to live after our own; but the great man is he who in the midst of the crowd keeps with perfect sweetness the independence of solitude.

The objection to conforming to usages that have become dead to you is that it scatters your force. It loses your time and blurs the impression of your character. If you maintain a dead church, contribute to a dead Bible-society, vote with a great party either for the government or against it, spread your table like base housekeepers, —under all these screens I have difficulty to detect the precise man

23

3. Margins too skimpy

The difference between men is in their principle of association. Some men classify objects by color and size and other accidents of appearance; others by intrinsic likeness, or by the relation of cause and effect. The progress of the intellect is to the clearer vision of causes, which neglects surface differences. To the poet, to the philosopher, to the saint, all things are friendly and sacred, all events profitable, all days holy, all men divine. For the eye is fastened on the life, and slights the circumstance. Every chemical substance, every plant, every animal in its growth, teaches the unity of cause, the variety of appearance.

Upborne and surrounded as we are by this all-creating nature, soft and fluid as a cloud or the air, why should we be such hard pedants, and magnify a few forms? Why should we make account of time, or of magnitude, or of figure? The soul knows them not, and genius, obeying its law, knows how to play with them as a young child plays with graybeards and in churches. Genius studies the casual thought, and far back in the womb of things sees the rays parting from one orb, that diverge, ere they fall, by infinite diameters. Genius watches the monad through all his masks as he performs the metempsychosis of nature. Genius detects through the fly, through the cater-

25

4. Margins too wide

Examples of badly designed pages

The Snow Goose

by PAUL GALLICO

NEW YORK : ALFRED · A · KNOPF

19 41

THE SNOW GOOSE

THE GREAT MARSH lies on the Essex coast between the village of Chelmbury and the ancient Saxon oyster-fishing hamlet of Wickaeldroth. It is one of the last of the wild places of

PAUL GALLICO

buffeted her about. It was a truly terrible storm, stronger than her great wings, stronger than anything. For days and nights it held her in its grip and there was nothing she could do but fly before it. When finally it had blown itself out and her sure instincts took her south again, she was over a different land and surrounded by strange birds that she had never seen before. At last, exhausted by her ordeal, she had sunk to rest in a friendly green marsh, only to be met by the blast from the hunter's gun.

"A bitter reception for a visiting princess," concluded Rhayader. "We will call her 'La Princesse Perdue,' the Lost Princess. And in a few days she will be feeling much better. See?" He reached into his pocket and produced a handful of

20

THE SNOW GOOSE

grain. The snow goose opened its round yellow eyes and nibbled at it.

The child laughed with delight, and then suddenly caught her breath with alarm as the full import of where she was pressed in upon her, and without a word she turned and fled out of the door.

"Wait, wait!" cried Rhayader, and went to the entrance, where he stopped so that it framed his dark bulk. The girl was already fleeing down the sea wall, but she paused at his voice and looked back.

"What is your name, child?"

"Frith."

"Eh?" said Rhayader. "Fritha, I suppose. Where do you live?"

21

A trade book, designed by Georg Salter

hance the appeal of a book, and a bad one can do quite a bit of damage. There are some publishers who engage designers to do only the front matter, to "dress up" a book which in other respects may be already completely planned. This is like getting one man, a builder, to build a house and then getting an architect to design a façade. This is not good practice because a really harmonious result is not possible by this method. Yet it still happens in building, and in books.

What remains to be done now is the designing of the binding and the jacket. These are often worked out by specialists; the jacket in particular is often entrusted to an experienced artist in that field. An attractive book jacket not only draws attention to the book but gives an honest impression of what is in the volume and can do much to help sell the book. This is pretty generally recognized by publishers. But too often jackets are produced which are intended to make a book seem more glamorous, or more sensational than it really is. Nor do all publishers believe it important that jacket, binding, and typography should really blend together in the way every good designer would like them to. If the designer is conscientious and serious about his job, he will have to make an extra effort to keep control of the job.

This is easier for him to do if he is working as a staff member of the publishing house in the manufacturing department, and especially if he combines the jobs of design and production. The free-lance designer is in a more difficult position as far as following up on his design is concerned. He may be lucky and get a chance to supervise the execution of his plans, but often he does not.

You may wonder perhaps why we have spent so much time watching the book designer at work. After all, there are many other men and women in the graphic arts field who render valuable services, such as highly skilled craftsmen, technicians, and engineers.

The reason for the special importance of the designer lies in his key position. He is in a favorable situation to control all the many separate operations. He not only coordinates these into a smooth-running production schedule, he also has the power to shape the book into a thing of beauty. It is he, more than any other person, who can see to it that the book which comes from the press is not only a readable presentation of the message of the author, not only an efficient instrument of information and communication, but something beyond that. He can instill into the book something of the spirit of human dignity. What would otherwise, without his services, be an impersonal technical product, a merely mechanical reproduction of words and pictures, can become in his hands a genuine expression of the human personality. In its own way, the well-designed book, like the well-built house, can help to make our world a better place to live in. In this way the book designer, instead of being the servant of the machine, can become its master.

Part III

HOW BOOKS ARE SOLD; SHOW THEY ARE READ AND COLLECTED

Chapter 12

BOOKSELLING

When the designer, the printer, and the binder have completed their work, the book is ready for the market. The author's manuscript has now become a printed book. Thousands of identical copies are shipped by the manufacturing plant to the publisher's office or his warehouse, ready to be sold. How are the books moved from there into the hands of the readers?

Many channels are open to the publisher, some of them developed quite recently in connection with the startling advances in communication and transportation; others dating back hundreds of years.

One of the oldest and most universal means of book distribution is door-to-door selling. In the olden days the traveling book salesman, called chapman or colporteur, carried with him books, pamphlets, tracts, and broadsides, often in a wooden container which was strapped to his back. He was able to penetrate to the lonely farmsteads off the beaten track and to the clearing in the wilderness. His services were important, for he was often the only source of reading matter for peasant and farmer in out-of-the-way places.

Everybody in America has heard of Johnny Appleseed. When he was roaming through the wilderness of Ohio, planting his appleseeds, he carried with him the writings of Emanuel Swedenborg, the Swedish seer who wrote down his frequent conversations with angels and spirits, from whom he learned about the world of the hereafter. Johnny Appleseed was very anxious that these messages should be read by everyone, but as he had no tract society to supply him with books, he devised an original method of multiplying one book into a number

Johnny Appleseed, chapman

of them. He divided his books into several pieces, leaving one portion at a log cabin on one visit and furnishing another fragment on a subsequent visit, continuing this process as diligently as though the work had been published in serial form. By this plan he was able to supply reading for several people at the same time—and out of one book. But it must have been a difficult undertaking for some nearly illiterate backwoodsman to try to understand Swedenborg by this somewhat backward course of reading, for his first installment could very well be the last fraction of the volume.[1]

Some years ago, the *Saturday Evening Post*[2] carried a story about a man called Ted Richmond, a penniless librarian, who for twenty years has trudged the Ozark back country to bring books to the people of the woods. Like Johnny Appleseed, he does not work for profit, for he gives his books away, content to serve his fellowmen. These men are, of course, exceptions, for door-to-door selling of books is usually a business by which a man has to make a living.

The prince of American chapmen early in the nineteenth century was Parson Weems, who peddled his books along the eastern seaboard between Pennsylvania and Georgia. He was so prosperous that he could afford horse and wagon to carry him and his wares. Many of

[1]Retold from *A Treasury of American Folklore*, edit. by B. A. Botkin, New York, Crown Publishers, 1944.

[2]"Modern Shepherd of the Hills," by Hartzell Spence, in the November 8, 1952 issue.

the books he sold had been written by himself, such as biographies of Washington, Franklin, and Penn. It was Parson Weems who created the story of the boy George Washington and the cherry tree.

Door-to-door selling of books is still practiced today under the name of subscription selling. You yourself may have been present when the salesman for an encyclopedia, *Book of Knowledge*, or the Bible has called on your family. The sets of books are usually sold on the installment plan, and radio and television programs, advertising in newspapers and in magazines, support and supplement the efforts of the salesman.

However, subscription selling is only one of many forms of bookselling. The publisher will use one or several methods of distributing his products, depending on the kind of book he has published and the reading public it is intended for.

Before the selling starts, the publisher announces the official retail price and the publication date of a new book, the day on which copies can begin to move from the various trade channels into the hands of the readers.

To give his new book a favorable start, the publisher will have planned an advertising and publicity campaign, using newspapers, magazines, the radio, and television.

He must also plan to get the book reviewed, which he does by sending advance copies to many newspapers and magazines, and directly to well-known reviewers and book columnists.

The publisher employs traveling salesmen who call on all the important bookstores. They carry with them a sample copy of the new book or a so-called sales dummy, which shows jacket, binding, and title and contents pages, and contains also a short explanation of what the book is about. When the bookseller thinks the book will bring him business, he will place his order for as many copies as he estimates he will need for a start. The publisher may also write letters to important booksellers about his new books, and he will advertise in special magazines, particularly in *Publishers' Weekly*, the leading American book trade journal.

The retail bookseller plays a very important part in launching a new book. He can make attractive window displays and send out announcements to his own list of customers. He may also give an autographing party, with the author present in the store as the guest of honor. But the bookseller's efforts cannot be spent only on a few outstanding new books which are heading for the top bestseller list. To satisfy the many demands of his customers, as well as their different tastes and interests, he must carry in stock a large assortment of books in many fields and from many different publishers.

Here is one of the most valuable services which the retail bookseller can render to his community: giving the book-buying public the opportunity to inspect a book before purchasing it. There is a great deal of satisfaction in making your own choice, comparing different books in the same field, reading their contents pages,

A bookshop today

looking at the pictures. An experienced and helpful staff, ready to answer questions and willing to take an interest in the individual customer, is a great asset to a bookseller who wishes to take a useful and productive part in the life of his community.

Unfortunately, running a bookstore as a profitable business is not an easy task these days. The bookstore owner, like the author and the publisher, can rarely count on making a living from selling books alone. He has no share in the extra income from the "subsidiary rights" (see page 38) which author and publisher divide between them. So he must get his additional income by carrying some other merchandise—stationery, gift items, or phonograph records.

A good bookstore needs the support of a fairly large community; it usually cannot succeed in cities with a population of less than 25,000, unless it is located in a suburb whose residents are fairly well off, or in a college community where a fair share in the profitable textbook business may be counted on. It is in the smaller university or college towns particularly where the "personal bookshop" can still stay in business. This is the kind of bookstore which is owned and run by an individual, or perhaps by two partners who share their financial resources, their experience, and love of books. In the large cities, chains of retail stores have become more and more general, like the Doubleday chain in New York; Burrows in Cleveland; Brentano's branches in the various cities; and Fred Harvey's chain in the West and Southwest.

Some bookstores are specialized, carrying only books in certain fields. Rare book stores, too, are in a class by themselves, and they are closely connected with book collecting, both by private individuals and libraries. We will return to the rare and second-hand bookstores in the next chapter, and a word will also be said there about the fascinating book auction game.

One thing is agreed upon by everyone who cares

about books and reading in America: there are not enough bookstores in this country. Large sections of the country are without them. The uneven distribution of the stores in different parts of the country is a characteristic feature of the American book trade. There are "strong" and "weak" regions which do not seem to change much throughout the years. The strong region extends along the Atlantic seaboard from Maine to New Jersey and west through Pennsylvania and Ohio, as far "out" as Wisconsin and Illinois, leaving Minnesota, Iowa, and Missouri as border territories. The other parts of the country, with the striking exceptions of California and Texas, are weak. This division can be observed not only in regard to the retail bookstores. The figures showing how much libraries spend on books per capita of the population, the distribution of rental libraries, the volume of subscription selling, all follow the same pattern.

Libraries, as a matter of fact, are among the most important customers for a new book, and many volumes are sold directly to them. The New York Public Library, for instance, ordered for its circulating department, which supplies the library's branches in all of Greater New York, over 1,200 copies of Wouk's *Marjorie Morningstar* in the first six months following publication, and over 900 copies of Thompson's *Not as a Stranger* in a period of twenty-one months.

Schoolbooks and textbooks are in a group by themselves, and they are often sold not through bookstores, but directly from the publisher to the educational system, to the various boards of education, and to the schools directly. Much the same thing is true of college textbooks, which, however, are also sold in college bookstores located on the campuses of many universities and colleges.

Bookstores and libraries do not always buy the books which they plan to sell or lend out over the counter directly from the publisher. They often send their orders to a wholesaler or book jobber. Such a firm carries in stock the books of many different publishers. This makes it possible for the bookstore owner to send to the wholesaler one order for books of perhaps five or six different publishers, instead of having to make out that many individual orders.

A publisher can and often does sell copies of a book directly to the customer. For instance, if a book is likely to be interesting or useful to one particular group, such as engineers, or sculptors, or botanists, the publisher will send circulars to the members of these professions. Coupon advertising is a device frequently used in this connection. The publisher's mailing piece may contain a small-sized order blank on a coupon which can be cut out and sent to the publisher. Coupon advertising is also used in some specialized magazines, and often in newspapers, particularly to promote inspirational and "How to do it" books.

One thing is certain about selling a book. No matter which method a publisher or bookseller may choose to promote a new title, the best salesmen any book can have are the people who read it and like it well enough to mention it to other people.

We must not forget to mention the book clubs, such as the Book-of-the-Month Club, the Literary Guild, the Story Classics, or such highly specialized clubs as the Art Book Guild of America, or the Yachtsmen's Book Club. Perhaps you are familiar, too, with the Teen-Age Book Club, sponsored by Scholastic Magazines.

You may become a member of a book club by signing an agreement that you will select a certain number of books each year from lists submitted by the book club. The subscriber agrees to buy a minimum number of different titles a year (six in the case of the Book-of-the-Month Club), and more if he wishes to do so. As a rule, book club prices are much below the official retail prices of the publisher. The book clubs can afford to sell at such low prices because they buy from the publisher large quantities of the books selected, or they purchase at a favorable price the right to print their own, large editions. Even if a book club charges the publisher's price for the monthly selections, the effect of a reduction in price is achieved through a special membership feature—free premium books, also called "book-dividends"— which are given at frequent intervals.

Book clubs started in Germany, some time after the First World War, and they were a great success there. When they were tried out in the United States, it turned out that here too book clubs worked very well. The new idea behind the book club is the use of a previously neglected communication network: the United States Post Office. By the use of the mails for advertising (direct mail advertising, it is called), books are brought to the attention of large groups of people in many parts of the country who have little or no contact with bookstores and libraries. By accepting orders and shipping books by mail, the book clubs render a valuable service. However, there has been some criticism of the ways in which books are selected by some of the clubs. It has been pointed out that the system is apt to lead to a concentration on only those books which have a very broad, popular appeal. There is some apprehension that in this way the choice of the reader becomes too limited and that there are many valuable, but not so popular, books which may not get the chance they deserve.

This difficulty exists also in connection with many of the paper-covered books which sell for 25, 35, 50, and occasionally 75 cents or more a copy in drugstores, on newsstands, from automatic vending machines, and through several other outlets.

In one way, these volumes have been a great blessing, in that they have brought books within the reach of millions who never before could have afforded to buy them. These books have revolutionized the reading habits of countless men, women, and children, who previously did not read at all, or read only newspapers and magazines. The paper-bound books have also made a place for themselves on the campuses, in the schools, and on the shelves of the public libraries. But the difficulty is that as a rule enormous quantities of each title have to be printed in order to produce a profit, and this has often favored the selection of the most popular and often rather shoddy and worthless kind of writing, to the disadvantage of books of more lasting value.

Perhaps you remember that in the chapter on publishing (page 32) we discussed the number of copies that are printed for the first edition of a regular trade book. This number has to be much higher in the inexpensive paper-bound books. Pocket Books, the pioneer in the field, and the other big concerns such as Bantam, Avon, and the New American Library, have to print no less than 200,000 copies of a new title if the publication is to be a sound economic venture. The smaller paper-book publishers can manage somewhat smaller printings.

Pocket Book's all-time bestseller is Dr. Benjamin Spock's *Pocket Book of Baby and Child Care*, which has sold, at the time this is written, about eight million copies. The *Merriam-Webster's Pocket Dictionary* (35 cents) has sold between four and five million copies.

I think these facts make it clear that the book of an author who does not appeal to an exceedingly large number of readers does not easily make the grade. Unfortunately it seems that the books liked by the largest number of people are usually superficial and sensational entertainment. There have been notable exceptions. Many publishers of paper books keep trying, often at heavy risks, to promote the better books. By a careful study of their lists it is possible to find these titles. Then, too, there are entire series containing only books of lasting value, affectionately known in the trade by the nickname "egghead series." The higher-priced paper books, which sell from 95 cents up to $1.25 through the regular book trade channels rather than on the newsstands, have many excellent titles.

The Kent School in Connecticut and other schools have been very successful with a Book Cafeteria. In their library are wire racks on which are displayed good books published by Pocket Books, the Mentor and Signet books of the New American Library, good titles from Bantam Books, the English Penguin Books, Anchor Books, Perma Books, and Ballantine Books. The students at Kent make good use of this opportunity to select and buy for themselves books of lasting value.

What do we mean when we speak of "books of lasting value"? I think this is rather an important question. No two people have exactly the same taste, and one of the most enjoyable things about books is that you can pick for yourself what you want to read. So we ought to talk a little more about the pleasure of reading and how you can get the most out of books.

Chapter 13

ON THE FINE ART OF READING

When you open a book and start reading, the author begins to talk to you. This is the moment he has been hoping for. For this he has labored countless hours of the day and the night. The fact that you are now setting out to read what he wants to tell you is his best reward.

Reading can be a very private and a very personal communication between two human beings. It is you the author is talking to. Behind the lines of type is the man or woman who wishes to speak to you. Sometimes in quiet reading you can almost hear the voice of the author.

Nor is this communication altogether a one-way affair. You are not just on the receiving end, taking in a message that comes to you from the printed page. One of the most delightful of the many ways of enjoying a book is the very leisurely reading of just a sentence or two, interrupted by your own thoughts, recollections, and anticipations. In this fashion reading can almost become a conversation. Naturally, the physical man or woman who is the author cannot hear your voice or read your mind at a distance. This is not what I mean. I mean that the thoughts he thinks, the feelings he feels, his experience and knowledge can make you think and feel and know things within yourself which you may not have had any idea were there. Reading, in other words, can help you to discover yourself, to awaken

The adventure of reading

you inside in ways which you might not have suspected.

This is the blessing of the art of quiet reading. Naturally, like the art of listening to music, or looking at pictures, it may not be yours all at once. It may take some time to discover some of these things. This quiet reading by yourself, reading slowly, even rereading a sentence or a page, or maybe a whole chapter can be very rewarding. There is an old saying that no book is worth reading once if it is not worth reading twice. This is of course not true of the books which you consult only for some kind of special information.

It sometimes takes a painful experience to learn about the blessing of reading. It has always seemed to me that just about the greatest unhappiness a human being can suffer is the feeling that in some mysterious and hostile way he has been singled out by misfortune. This feeling that you, and you alone, seem to have been burdened with some particular kind of unhappiness can be very painful. No one among your family, or friends, or acquaintances seems to have anywhere near such unhappiness to carry around and, what's more, no one seems to notice your troubles or care about them particularly. But if you are lucky, chance may place into your hands a book which tells you of just such trouble in someone else's life and how he or she mastered it. This may sound to you like a very strange coincidence, but it happens much more often than you might think.

A book can be a real friend. It can keep you company when you are lonely, help pass the time away when you are bored, give you answers to questions which may be puzzling you, teach you to know and understand other people, and make you a better friend to someone who may need your help. But unlike many of your human friends, the book makes no demands on you. You can stop reading, close the covers, and put the book away whenever you feel like it. It will be ready and waiting for you when you are ready for it again.

Mind you, the way in which a book may help you does not depend on the story being an exact counterpart of your own experience or a literal anticipation of it. Behind your own experience is more than you alone, more than your immediate family or community, or job or human relations. You want to understand that the same thing is true of the people you are reading about in the book. The author has to bring his characters alive in their own experiences and surroundings. But he does this in order to express something beyond the individual character and the individual experience. He wants to reach back into the broader, more general happenings, into the more subtle and deeper experiences of people in this world. He knows that he must bring this about if he wishes his writing to be important and meaningful for the thousands of single readers who make up his audience.

What is important is not only what a writer says, but also how he says it.

Some of the most important things in human lives cannot easily be expressed in words. If you do not believe this, try to tell in words the truly important things about a dream you may have had some night, or what happiness really feels like, or sadness, or love.

The thing that distinguishes the author from other kinds of people is his special ability to use words. A great writer has it in his power to express for us ideas and feelings which are familiar to many of us but which we may never have been able to describe to others. The writer can say these things for us in ways which make them understandable. This can be a great relief and the source of much new courage and strength.

Books can also help you look into the future. How? By showing you the past. This is not meant as a joke. Nor am I trying to tell you in all seriousness that you can look up in books what is going to happen next week, or next Christmas, or after your twenty-first birthday. Such fortune-telling books do exist, but I have not found them very reliable. I mean something else.

We do wish to look ahead. This is not only natural but also necessary. What we should try to find out about is the possibilities ahead of us, the varieties of things that may come to pass. We should try to learn about the issues in the life of our nation, in foreign relations, in domestic policies; what problems industry and labor are facing; what kind of training will be useful in the years ahead; what diseases, physical and mental, are being fought and by what means; what kinds of inventions lie ahead, and so on.

In every attempt to look ahead, knowledge of what

has already happened is of the greatest value. The person who has some insight into the past experiences of mankind, no matter in what particular field, has a much better chance of preparing for the future than the person who ignores the past. Books are the key to the vast riches of the experiences that lie behind us.

There are many ways of unlocking this treasure house. You may choose your own personal guide in the person of an author of our own time who has traveled into the land of the past and can tell you in his writings what he has found there. Or you can explore for yourself. Through the medium of the book you can invite a man or a woman from any land of the globe and from any time within the last 2,000 years or so to come into your home and speak to you. Your guest can be an emperor or a beggar, a Chinese or a Scot, a wise man or a fool, a happy person or a sad one. He will stay as long as he is welcome, leave when you want him to leave, and come back again if you so desire.

The book in your hand is indeed the key to riches of which you need never tire.

SOME HINTS ON HOW TO GET ACQUAINTED WITH A BOOK

The art of reading, like any other art, has its technical side which it is worth knowing about. I would like to put down here a few things which may be helpful to you in your living with books.

It is very useful to know how to find out quickly what a book is about. The volume which you pick up in the library or bookstore, if it is a new book, will probably have the publisher's jacket on it. The jacket will tell you the title of the book and probably the name of the author. On the back or the inside flaps the publisher often prints useful information about the author and the contents of the book. In many cases the jacket will also have a picture which is intended to arouse your interest and curiosity. You cannot always rely on the impression which you may get from the jacket. It is better to turn to the title page.

On the title page you will find again the name of the author, the name of the book, the name of the illustrator (if any), the place where it was published, the name of the publisher, and sometimes the date of publication. The title page will also tell you if the book is translated from a foreign language and who made the translation. In books of information and of a scientific and scholarly nature, you may find a brief line telling you what institution an author is connected with, and also the names of any collaborators who may have helped prepare the volume. When a book is by a new or little-known writer, some famous person may have written a special introduction, and that too is noted on the title page. The name of the publisher on the title page may not mean anything to you at first, but you will soon become familiar with the names of some of the great publishing houses. It is of course possible that the book is a second, third, etc. edition. That too, is often noted on the back of the title page where you may find information about when the book was first published (so you can see at a glance how recent the book is) and how many copies have been printed so far. From this you can learn how popular it is or has been.

The contents page is very important, especially in a book of information. With a little practice you can learn a great deal from reading the contents page. Here is the best place to discover what the book really covers, how well it is organized, how easy to use. A vaguely worded contents page is often an indication of a poor book.

Next, take a look at the preface or the introduction, if there is one or the other, or both. Most authors usually say in one or two sentences why they wrote the book, what their purpose was. This statement is often the key to the entire volume. With a little practice it is not difficult to find this key statement.

Illustrations, too, are important clues, easily discovered by quickly turning the leaves. They may be scattered throughout the text, or grouped together. Looking at the pictures is an excellent way of discovering what the book is about. It may help you to find out how the subject has been treated, whether imaginatively or factually, in a broad general way, or with emphasis on some special things.

Look also for other features, such as maps, tables of data, diagrams, musical notation. See if there are footnotes, either at the bottom of the pages, at the end of chapters, or at the end of the book. Look in those same places for lists of titles of the books, articles, and other sources which the author has used in his preparation or which he recommends to the reader. All this material is most helpful in your first, quick examination. It will not take you long in this way to discover if the book is something you want to read or not.

This idea of rapidly examining a book without actually reading it may surprise some of you, and you may wonder if it is really a good approach. True enough, if somebody has little or no previous acquaintance with books, it would be best not to judge too hastily. But a little practice, a little experimenting, goes a long way.

To do full justice to a book and to get the most out of it, one ought to read it through, of course. But there is nothing wrong with a little sampling here and there, in order to get acquainted with a book. If one opens a volume at random and begins to read whatever happens to meet the eye, the first sentence or two may not mean very much. But the reading of a paragraph or two soon will make sense. Testing a book by "tasting" samples here and there is a good way of becoming quickly acquainted. There are so many new books being published all the time, and so many old books waiting to be read, that it is a good idea to learn how to find your way to those which really have something to say to you.

Many factual, or "nonfiction" books, as they are

usually called, have an index at the back. A well-made index can be a great help to the reader, in first getting acquainted and also in subsequent reading or consultation of a volume. A typical general index is arranged alphabetically. It lists the names of persons and places mentioned in the text. It also lists the most important subjects dealt with by the author in much the way subjects are listed in an encyclopedia or dictionary. An index makes it possible to use a book for reference without necessarily having to read the whole of it or even entire chapters. If you want to find out as much as possible about an important person, or a country or town, or about any special topic of particular interest to you, the index will show you at a glance if the book has any of the information which you are looking for.

Chapter 14

ON THE JOYS OF BOOK COLLECTING

Book collecting is a hobby which can be enjoyed by anybody, whether man or woman, old or young, rich or poor. Building a private library is a source of steady satisfaction which can last a lifetime. There are many different ways of becoming a collector.

One of the most natural approaches is through reading. A friend may give you a book written by an author, living or dead, whom he believes you will like. You find that he was right, and you want to read something else written by the same person, so you buy a second book to read and put on a shelf alongside the first. In time you add other books by the same author. The same process may repeat itself with another writer, and it will not take long for you to assemble a nice shelf full of books you have enjoyed reading and would like to read again and, perhaps, lend to some of your friends.

Possibly your favorite author has aroused your curiosity about some special topic, such as the way of life of people in faraway places or long ago, or the achievements of some great inventor or artist. You hear of books about this same topic written by other people, and you add some of these volumes to your growing library.

Perhaps one of your volumes has some particularly interesting or beautiful pictures in it. The name of the illustrator is mentioned in the book, and you look around for other books illustrated by the same artist. Or you discover that one of your favorite story books has been illustrated at different times by different artists, and you try to get together some of these various editions.

Next you discover that even without pictures there are such differences in various editions of the same book that you try to assemble on your shelf as many editions as you can. Of course, the more time that has elapsed since the book was first published, the more different editions will have been published. For instance, if you would like to collect different editions of Lewis Carroll's *Alice in Wonderland*, first published in 1865, you have a little less than a century to select from. By contrast, there is *Praise of Folly*, by Desiderius Erasmus of Rotterdam, which was first published in Basle in 1515. This book is full of the kind of wisdom and humor that has appealed to readers ever since. Recent editions were published in Princeton in 1941 and in Chicago in 1946. So there are nearly four hundred years to select from. If you happen to be interested in foreign languages, you can include translations in your collection. *Alice in Wonderland*, for instance, was translated from the original English into more than a dozen foreign languages, and *Praise of Folly* has appeared in Latin, English, German, French, Italian, Spanish, Russian, and Czech translations.

When the day comes that you acquire a first edition, you are on your way to exploring an entirely new and fascinating field. As in stamp collecting, the question whether the volume at hand is really the first edition depends sometimes on very small details, such as one or two uncorrected typographical errors somewhere in the text, or whether or not an engraved plate has the name of the artist on it, or on the color and pattern of the cloth binding.

Speaking of bindings, you will soon discover the amazing varieties of materials and colors used to protect and decorate books. Your earliest acquisition will probably be the current paper backs and the "hard-cover" cloth bindings on the trade books of today. As time goes on, some nineteenth-century "Victorian" cloth binding, slightly faded perhaps, but with the gold stamping still fresh, will appear, soon to be joined by some older "half-leather" volumes, the backs covered with gilt-stamped leather, the boards with some nice old patterned paper pasted over them. The acquisition of his first full-leather binding, old or new, is a red-letter day for the collector. Some day, a venerable medieval volume, bound in parchment or vellum or in heavy wooden boards with pigskin-covered back, may be yours.

Well-arranged shelves of books can add a great deal of atmosphere to your home, and the day may come when you select a volume chiefly because of the interest and beauty of its binding.

To give fullest satisfaction, bindings need some care. "A stitch in time saves nine" is a good thing to remember. Regular application of some leather preservative (as sold by some bookstores) is a wise precaution. Beware also of the excessive dry heat produced by some heating systems. Following the very humid heat of our summers, this dry heat is as harmful to old books as it is to the breathing organs of human beings.

One of the nice things about collecting is the complete freedom to do as one pleases and to follow one's own inclinations. There is no need to hurry. A person can choose his own pace, adding a book every week, every month, or whenever he feels like it and whenever a good opportunity presents itself. A collection, once started, does not disappear. The books are there, waiting, ready for your attention when you have the time and inclination to turn to them.

There are countless ways in which one book or one group of books will lead to another book or another group of books. A growing library has a tendency to branch out, like a tree, sending out shoots in many directions which grow stronger from year to year and in time will send out new branches. Like a gardener, the collector can allow his library to grow freely in many directions, or he can cut out certain branches, thereby causing fewer but stronger limbs to develop. If he so pleases, a collector can limit himself to a specialty. Experience has shown that the more highly a book collection is specialized, the sooner it may become recognized as a leading collection in its particular field.

I said at the beginning of this chapter that there were many different ways of becoming a collector. A shelf full of practical reference books in the office or home of a professional man—doctor, lawyer, stage designer, or chemist—can hardly be called a real book collection, but it is a good starting point for one. Some very fine collections have begun that way, such as Dr. Harvey Cushing's great library on the history of medicine, now at Yale University, or Dr. David Eugene Smith's collection on the history of mathematics, now at Columbia University. The printed catalogs of these and of many other familiar collections are useful and important reference tools, not only for other collectors and book dealers, but also for librarians, scholars, and scientists.

Some people become book collectors simply because they like to collect things. They may have had other collections—stamps, toy soldiers, butterflies, coins. They may discover that book collecting offers them some special rewards and some special satisfaction. Pride of ownership enters into the picture, of course, as well as the interesting people who are fellow book collectors. Talking about one's prized possessions, telling of surprising discoveries, comparing notes on bargain hunting, making plans for the future, discovering other collections and bookshops and auctions—these topics offer plenty of opportunity for good conversation among booklovers.

Investing one's money in good books is also a motive in collecting. There are, of course, ups and downs in the book market as in every other market, and to some extent the tastes of collectors are subject to change. However, by and large, it can be stated that a well-chosen, well-developed, and well-cared-for private library is a sound investment.

BIG TREES FROM LITTLE ACORNS GROW

It is high time for us to discuss the financial side of book collecting. No great funds are necessary to start a private library. If a young person begins early in life, selecting wisely with some sense of purpose and direction and investing the same proportion of his spending money throughout the years, a most creditable and worth-while collection will be the result.

Perhaps this statement needs a little clarification. At the start, a young book collector may not be able to spend more than a dollar or so a month, or somewhere between ten and twenty dollars the first year or two. But the same percentage of his expendable income would soon grow to perhaps fifty or a hundred dollars a year, sufficient to bring some very desirable items within his reach. At this point he may decide to buy fewer and more valuable books within a given period.

There are no limits to the amounts that can be spent. I know a number of book collectors with practically unlimited purchasing ability, but whose experience and judgment never cease to guide their collecting activities along the path they have laid out for themselves.

The interest and value of a collection does not come solely from the rarities. They lie to a considerable extent in the varieties of materials brought together around one or two central ideas and in the imagination with which a plan has been pursued. It does not matter much what the subject of the collection may be. I never fail to marvel at the relatively short time in which persistence, enthusiasm, and ingenuity can make a collection grow. There are many types of publications, such as exhibition catalogs, pamphlets, and reprints which cost little or nothing at the time they are published; but they are often very difficult or actually impossible to find later on. Then, too, a growing collection of books seems to generate a kind of magnetism, which attracts other volumes. Gifts, bequests, and all sorts of unexpected opportunities develop quite frequently and often in the most unexpected fashion.

ABOUT THE RARE BOOK TRADE

In the normal course of events book purchasing for a private library will start at the regular retail channels for currently published books, as they have been described in the chapter on bookselling (pages 159 to 171). Gradually, more specialized sources of supply will enter the picture.

The rare and second-hand bookshops are the haunts of the true collector. There are many of these stores, and they are all quite different from each other, depending on their location, the tastes and talents of the owner, and, in the cases of stores established long ago, the particular traditions of a given firm. Not all of the stores combine the "second-hand" and the "rare book" business. In New York City, for instance, lower Fourth Avenue is a paradise for bargain hunters, and out-of-print books are offered for prices as low as ten or twenty-five cents a volume. In some of the midtown New York rare book stores, it would be difficult to find many books selling for less than fifteen or twenty dollars each.

Some very large amounts of money have been spent for rare books. For instance, a copy of the Gutenberg Bible, once in the possession of the Monastery of Melk in Austria, sold for $100,000 in 1926. Copies of the famous "first folio" edition of Shakespeare's plays have brought between $15,000 and $40,000. The *Bay Psalm Book*, "the first thing in English America that can be called a book" (George Parker Winship in *The Cambridge Press*), has sold for as much as $151,000 for a single copy. In 1955, a copy of George Washington's *Journal*, printed at Williamsburg, sold for $25,000.

Much book collecting and rare book buying is done by mail through dealers' catalogs. A considerable number of rare and second-hand dealers in this country and in England, as well as on the Continent, issue catalogs. They range all the way from inexpensively produced mimeographed sheets to beautifully printed and illustrated volumes, which are collectors' items in themselves. These catalogs are mailed by the dealers to their regular customers and librarians, to the members of book collectors' clubs, and to scholars and scientists who may be interested in the contents of a given catalog.

To get on these mailing lists is usually quite easy. A postcard requesting a dealer's latest catalogs and stating your fields of interest is often sufficient.[1]

To stay on these mailing lists is sometimes not so easy. If a dealer never gets an order from a customer, he will become discouraged.

One other important source of supply for the collector should be mentioned: the book auction room.

Buying books at an auction can be a very exciting game. The books are sold one by one by the auctioneer to the highest bidder. Competition is sometimes very keen, and fabulous prices have been paid for choice items. At other times, the bidding may be sluggish, and really desirable items may be sold at far below their true value. There is a decided element of chance, and no one can tell ahead of time how things will go at any one sale.

[1] A good place to inquire for the names of rare and second-hand dealers is your local library. The classified directory of the telephone company also lists some names.

Anybody can buy at a book auction, and both collectors and dealers are found at the auction room. But it is not necessary to attend in person. Printed catalogs are issued and mailed out in advance of each auction, and a collector in Cincinnati or New Orleans can send in his bid to the auctioneer in New York, London, Paris, or Geneva. Of course, he will have to decide ahead of time how high he is willing to go. He will not be able to change his mind the way a buyer on the spot may do when the auction room fever gets hold of him. Many collectors prefer to do their bidding through trusted dealers present at the sale. Some lively bidding among two or three dealers may be on behalf of faraway collectors whose names may never become known.

To a newcomer the goings-on in an auction room can appear to be very mysterious. The auctioneer calls out in rapid succession bids for ever-higher amounts which he receives seemingly from nowhere. Suddenly his gavel hits the desk, and the item is knocked down to an invisible customer. The reason for this is that many buyers, although they may be most eager for an item, like to appear very detached and, if possible, let no one but the auctioneer know that they are bidding. So they often work by previously arranged secret signals, such as holding their pencil a certain way, or touching their chin in a manner which the other buyers cannot notice.

Most books sold at auction come from collectors who, for one reason or another, wish to sell certain portions or all of their collections, or from estates of deceased collectors which have to be liquidated. The advantage of selling books at auction is that in this fashion they can be disposed of rather promptly and for cash. The disadvantages lie in the element of chance, since there can be no assurance ahead of time what the bidding will be like. However, good items, by and large, can be said to bring fair prices.

WHAT MAKES A BOOK RARE?

"What makes a book rare?" is one of the questions most frequently asked of anyone who has to do with rare books. Whenever a collector, dealer, or curator gets his name in the papers, he inevitably receives letters from all sorts of people telling him about the old family Bible in the attic and asking how much it may be worth. Ninety times out of a hundred there is no value other than the sentimental value to the owner himself and, perhaps, his immediate family. Occasionally, however, the search in the attic does pay off.

Perhaps the most famous case which happened in this part of the world concerns a copy of the first edition of Edgar Allan Poe's *Tamerlane*, first published in 1827. Only three copies of this very rare and highly desirable collector's item were known to exist. In the midsummer of 1925[1] Vincent Starrett published a story in the *Saturday Evening Post* called "Have you a *Tam-*

[1] As told by Charles E. Goodspeed of Boston in his *Yankee Bookseller*, Boston, 1937.

erlane in your attic?" in which he told how a copy of this slim little volume had sold for $10,000. This story was read by a Mrs. Dodd, in Worcester, Massachusetts, who lived in rather straitened circumstances with her aged sister. It so happened that Mrs. Dodd was living in an attic and she did have a *Tamerlane*. In due course she received $14,000 for her book from Mr. Goodspeed, to whom she had entrusted the volume, and who sold it to Owen D. Young for $17,500.

Contrary to many people's notion, mere age does not make for rarity, and the alluring fact that the pages are tattered and torn and browned with age and the bindings in shreds detracts further from the possible value of many an old volume. The literal meaning of the word "rare," indicating that something is scarce, hard to find, is a better key to its potential value.

Some old books or pamphlets are rare because when they first appeared on the market they were much in demand, read by many persons, passed on from hand to hand, and used up in the process. Christopher Columbus' famous letter of 1493, in which he announced his discovery of certain new islands to the west to the treasurer of King Ferdinand of Aragon, is a good example. Another one is the Latin school grammar of a Roman grammarian named Donatus, first printed in Mainz soon after the invention of printing—very rare indeed and surviving in but a few copies and fragments.

In the nineteenth century some of the great novels by Dickens, Thackeray, and other famous writers were first published in parts, which appeared at more or less regular intervals. It is easy to see how some of these installments might readily go astray. That is why a complete set of, for instance, Dickens' *Pickwick Papers*, with all the parts present in good condition in their charmingly decorated paper wrappers, is a desirable collector's item.

First editions are often much rarer than any of the later editions because the printer or publisher may have underestimated the book's chances for success and printed far too few copies to go around. Another reason for the rarity of a first edition may be that a book ran into trouble with the authorities and was suppressed, even burned, or had to be reprinted with certain alterations. An interesting French book on America, for instance, Henri de Tonty's *Account of Monsieur La Salle's last expedition and discoveries in America* appeared first in Paris in 1697. In its rare first printing it contained several pages of information on the pearl fisheries in the Mississippi delta. The French authorities thought it wise to suppress this information, so the pages in question had to be reprinted.

Beautifully printed and illustrated books can become rare because they are desirable as examples of the art of the book, eagerly collected by people who enjoy owning fine books, as well as by libraries and museums which need such works for exhibition and study purposes. Then, too, such books are sometimes expressly printed in small editions at fairly high prices for sale by subscription or for members of such organizations as the Limited Editions Club in New York.

Experience has shown that a rare book cannot be deliberately created. No matter when, where, and how a book is printed and published, it has to make its own way and stand on its own feet, so to speak.

The presence of a fine binding on an old rare volume, created by a recognized master of the craft, can add substantially to the value of a book. Fine bindings are judged by a number of different points: the technical excellence of a binding as a protective cover; the ease with which it can be opened; its ability to stand up to frequent use; the choice of good and attractive materials; the taste of the decorations and the lettering; and the condition of the binding—how well preserved it is, whether it is repaired or partially restored. These are the scoring points for a fine binding.

Still another reason for rarity is the presence of handwritten notes—the author's dedication to a friend or patron, written in his own hand, for example, or notes in the margin by some famous person who read the book when it first came out, or the marks of ownership of a great collector or library of the past.

Finally it should be mentioned that the law of supply and demand has a decided influence on the value of a rare book, as it has on any other marketable commodity. Tastes in book collecting do change somewhat over the years, and this has some effect on the desirability and hence the financial value of certain kinds of books.

However, there are a few broadly recognized fields of collecting which are not very much affected by changing fashions. It can be said that for the last hundred years in America the following kinds of books have been in more or less steady demand: medieval manuscripts, important both as works of art for the beauty of their illumination and calligraphy, and for their textual content; incunabula, the books printed in the fifteenth century, monuments of the infancy of the typographic art; Americana, including books printed anywhere and in any language on the discovery, conquest, settlement, and early history of North and South America, as well as the early books printed in America itself; English literature from Chaucer to Shakespeare and Milton and on to the first editions of nineteenth- and twentieth-century authors; books of all periods printed by famous presses and remarkable as works of art because of the interest and beauty of their typography, decoration, illustration, and binding; also the special field of books about books. More recently, the "Heralds of Science" have come into their own, namely the books recording first discoveries and significant progress in man's conquest of the physical universe and reflecting the triumphs of science and technology in the modern world.

Many of the finest collections in any of the fields here mentioned are now the proud possessions of American libraries, monuments to the generosity and foresight of the great collectors of the last three generations. Through the fact of their donation to free public libraries or to colleges and universities, these collections are made accessible to an ever-widening circle of readers, students, and booklovers.

Chapter 15

A BRIEF NOTE ON LIBRARIES

Both the public libraries and the college and university libraries in America have benefited greatly from the generous gifts and bequests of private collectors. As far as their old and rare book treasures are concerned, some of our great libraries could almost be called collectors of collections. Thanks largely to the initiative, ambition, and foresightedness of individual benefactors, they have been able to catch up remarkably well, so that they often compare quite favorably with some of the great European libraries. In any comparison of book treasures here and abroad it must not be forgotten that the American libraries are often quite "young" institutions. Their beginnings in many instances do not go back beyond the last century, whereas some of the great European libraries have roots that reach back into the Middle Ages.

As an institution, the library is probably as old as the book itself. In thinking about the beginnings of libraries, the old question of what a book is comes up again. If we accept cuneiform tablets and papyrus rolls as books, then we can say that libraries existed in ancient Mesopotamia in the third millennium before Christ, in Egypt about 1,500 years before Christ (if not earlier), and later on in ancient Greece and Rome. Of the great libraries in Alexandria and in Pergamum we have already spoken (pages 52 and 57).

From the early Middle Ages, after the fall of the Roman Empire, and up to the beginnings of the universities toward the end of the medieval period, the libraries in the monasteries had a particularly important function. They were not only the centers of learning and of literary culture, but also the only existing organization for the production of books. Libraries at all times have had a great influence on new writing, and many books published today could not have been written without the aid of modern libraries. But the unique importance of the library in the medieval monastery lay in the fact that there was no other regular outside agency for the writing, copying, and distributing of manuscripts, which were of course the only kinds of books then in existence.

It is noteworthy that some of the medieval libraries have survived to the present day in the very localities where they were started. Also, some very old collections of manuscripts and early printed books have survived as groups, not necessarily in the libraries where they were first collected, but as recognizable parts of other libraries into which they were absorbed at one time or another.

Speaking very generally, it can be stated that the growth of libraries outside the monasteries became significant at about the time when the copying of manuscripts began to be practiced outside the monasteries. The rise of the European universities from the thirteenth century on favored the establishment of a regular book trade in these communities (as we have seen earlier, see page 71). The student, the teacher, the scholar could begin to own and develop a personal library, which in many cases would later be absorbed by a university or

A library of the past

other kind of institutional library, just as is happening in the twentieth century. The invention of printing, the availability of more and cheaper books of all kinds, gave, of course, a mighty impetus to the growth of various types of libraries.

In emphasizing the new possibilities which presented themselves to the individual book collector at the end of the Middle Ages, I do not mean to suggest that personal initiative, thirst for knowledge, and love of books were altogether absent before then. It is likely that at almost all periods in history there were individuals who brought together collections of books which eventually could grow into important permanent libraries. The only thing is that in the time before books became more readily available through fast multiple copying and then through printing, a privileged position in life was necessary to enable a man to collect books. He had to be a high dignitary of the Church, or the member of a wealthy and noble family, a statesman, or a prince, king, or emperor.

The libraries of European monarchs may have begun as private collections, the personal property of the head of the state. However, they gradually assumed a more public status. This was due partly to the steady growth of these collections, which were often handed down to the son and heir to the throne. The royal library also became the place to which authors, printers, and publishers would send their new books as a kind of voluntary and sometimes imposed tribute. A separate building often became necessary to house the ever-growing collections of books, and an appointed librarian and his staff were needed for their care. First a privileged few and gradually a widening circle of members of the court, government officials, scholars, and professional men were permitted to use the royal library. Eventually, the royal library became the country's National Library, although it is still called the Royal Library in most European countries which are ruled by a king.

The United States has its national library in the Library of Congress, founded at the beginning of the last century, when Washington, D. C. was chosen as the seat of the Federal Government. Created to serve the needs of the legislators, the Library of Congress has grown into one of the largest and most important libraries of the world. It has rich collections in many different fields and is the central collecting point for books published in this country. For over a century the law has required copyrighted books to be deposited in the Library, and since 1870 the registration of copyrights has been under the care of the Librarian of Congress. The Library has developed unique central facilities and services for bibliographical information which are available to everyone. The Library of Congress, it should be understood, is by no means among the oldest libraries in America. This honor belongs to the colleges, and to Harvard in particular, which got its name from the Reverend John Harvard, who in 1638 bequeathed to the college his library and half of his estate. The Yale College Library may almost be said to have preceded the establishment of the college. There is the tradition that each member of a group of ministers who were considering the establishment of a college in Connecticut in 1700 brought some books to the meeting, laying them on the table with the words: "I give these books for the founding of a college in this country."[1] Like Harvard, it received its name from the donor of the library, named Elihu Yale, an official of the East India Company.

Among the other college libraries started during the Colonial period are those of the College of William and Mary at Williamsburg, Virginia; the Library of King's College, now Columbia University, in New York City; the University of Pennsylvania; Princeton University (first called the College of New Jersey); and Dartmouth College, at Hanover, New Hampshire.

College and university libraries in America are perhaps not very different from similar libraries in other parts of the world, particularly in England. But the American public library has a character all its own. The free public library in large and small American cities is an institution that has no equal in other countries. It is an important part of our democratic society, and it belongs among its most characteristic features.

Of course, towns and cities in other countries of the world have their municipal libraries, but very often

[1] Ruth Shepard Granniss in *The Book in America*, New York, 1939, p. 360.

Reading room in a public library today

these are scholarly research libraries for the use of a rather limited circle of educated readers; they often house specialized collections on the local history of the town and its region. Only in recent years have these libraries opened their doors to the general public. The needs of the working class people in Europe are often catered to in special popular reading rooms, sometimes under a different administration from the town library.

The interesting and important thing about the public library in America is that it offers free reading facilities and a great number of varied services to every member of the community, young or old, rich or poor, regardless of race, color, or creed. Its doors are open to the highly educated as well as to the average reader, to the citizen and the immigrant, to persons in search of practical or special information as well as to those who wish to broaden their education generally and enrich their minds. The public library is host to the person who wishes to while away an idle hour as well as to the professional author and the scholar. Every day many thousands of people in the United States use their public library without ever realizing how privileged they are in comparison with the citizens of many other countries.

The American public library of today is the outgrowth of several kinds of institutions which originally differed a good deal from each other. For instance, the first public library in Boston, founded in 1653, must have been very much like a European library. It consisted of a "town house," with "a library and gallery for divines and scholars to meet in." Also, in the nineteenth century, a number of libraries for missionaries were started in America, as well as in England and Wales, by the Reverend Thomas Bray, founder of the Society for the Propagation of the Gospel in Foreign Parts. Almost automatically, these libraries took on a broader public character, and they became what was then called "lending laymen's libraries."

Next came the subscription libraries, for the use of small groups of people, each of whom would pay annual dues or buy stock in the library. But the payments were not very large, and soon non-subscribers were permitted to use these libraries, which belong among the important ancestors of the modern public library. It was none other than Benjamin Franklin who founded the first and most famous subscription library, namely the Library Company of Philadelphia, which is still going strong.

Early in the nineteenth century there came into being the various mercantile, young men's, and mechanics' libraries, the results of a broadening movement for popular education and a recognition of the workingman's right and duty to educate himself.

> "It was in the atmosphere of the early Republic, with its fervid struggling conditions and its bright, new revolutionary thought, that the public library had its birth. Slowly, under the impact of this idea—and a profoundly upsetting one it was—this most cloistered institution of the ages began gradually, reluctantly, to open its doors to the new, stirring world about. Through the tense, exciting years of the growing industrial age, with the change from a rural to an urban civilization, with the influence of Europe's underprivileged myriads, eager for a chance in this new world, with the doors of opportunity opening, and all America alive with confidence and swagger, the public library made a quiet, steady advance."[1]

The first American public library to be patterned along the lines which are generally accepted today was the Boston Public Library. In 1848 the Massachusetts General Court empowered the city of Boston to raise money by yearly taxation for the support of a public

[1] Ernestine Rose, *The Public Library in American Life*, New York, Columbia University Press, 1954, p. 26.

library, which in fact was founded in 1852—the first large city library to be organized as a municipal institution, free and open to the public.

The New York Public Library, as we know it today, is the result of the consolidation of three great libraries. In 1848 John Jacob Astor left $400,000 for the establishment of a public library "to be accessible at all reasonable hours and times for general use, free of expense to persons resorting thereto." In 1870 the famous book collector, James Lenox, presented his library to the public. Samuel Tilden, who died in 1886, provided in his will a trust "with capacity to establish and maintain a free library and reading room." In May 1895 the agreement of consolidation was signed.

Among the many great public libraries established in the course of the last hundred years one might mention those in Philadelphia, Baltimore, Detroit, Cleveland, Chicago, Cincinnati (with an especially beautiful modern building), Milwaukee, St. Louis, Dallas, and Los Angeles. However, there are many other public libraries in large and small communities, as well as various privately endowed and specialized libraries.

The central idea behind the modern public library is its capacity to serve as a "social intelligence center," to use the words of Melvil Dewey, one of the great leaders of the library profession in the last century.

"The librarian's purpose is to stir the public mind with the thoughts of many, to offer alternatives, to expand perspectives and widen the choices. If he does anything less, the high principle of the institution is isolated. . . . His professional skill in enticing the customers into the stacks, the peculiar mark of the public library worker today, is very different from the skill and the concern of the propagandist who . . . tries to get the citizen to read official statements of authoritarian truth. . . ."[1]

Here lies the crucial importance of the public library in the American democracy of today. The core of our political life is a government elected by the people in voluntary, free elections in which every adult man and woman can participate. This privilege carries with it a great responsibility for the individual citizen, namely that he must try to keep himself informed on what is going on at home and abroad. His education is not completed when he graduates from high school or college, and newspaper reading alone does not constitute a well-balanced mental diet. The public library has long recognized its opportunity as an adult education center. It has not only opened its doors to the people at large but has made a particular effort to attract readers from the many special groups that make up the communities which it serves. The library is "trying to meet in its own way and with its own resources the needs of the poor, the semi-literate, the underprivileged, and the groping masses of people"[2] who live at its door. The library has gone out of its way to reach the foreign-born, those who

[1] Lyman Bryson, in the foreword to Ernestine Rose's book, cited on page 206.

[2] Ernestine Rose in the book cited above.

speak languages other than English, the various national and racial groups, and the blind. It caters to various professional groups and trades. It is doing this not only by making its existing resources as easily available as possible, but also by developing various kinds of special collections, by distributing these geographically through a network of branches, and by providing adaptable and specially trained staffs.

Most likely, the readers of these pages are already familiar with some of the numerous ways in which the public library has opened its doors to children and young people. This has not always been the case. Just like many adults who use our free public libraries, children and teenagers may take all the present opportunities very much for granted without asking for the reasons why and how these things have come to be provided for them so liberally.

Speaking very generally, the reasons for the existence of children's rooms, of departments for work with young people, and for the various forms of cooperation between libraries and schools, are the same ones which lie behind the writing and publishing of this book. It is the realization that books and reading are precious things which have something to offer to human beings living today which other forms of information and entertainment are not able to provide. It is therefore of great importance for the shaping of the future that books may be allowed to continue their unique and special services.

It is very desirable that they do not suffer too much neglect in comparison with the many other things pressing for attention today.

For the library to offer special services to children and young people is one important way of introducing books into the lives of the present and of future generations. This is also a natural consequence of the thought that the American public library, in order to be as effective as possible, must try to reach as many special groups as possible and provide the answers to the special needs of these various groups.

Forerunners of the children's rooms in public libraries were the Sunday School libraries developed in England in the late eighteenth century. Salisbury, Connecticut, was a notable American pioneer with a collection of books for children dating back as far as 1803. With the founding of the American Library Association in 1876 the desirability of children's rooms became generally recognized.

"It is probable that the first actual separate children's room was established in New York in 1885, at the initiative of a public school teacher. . . . By 1900 children's rooms had become a natural part of a modern public library, and special training was being given for children's librarians. In more than one library, to be sure, the separate room for children was grudgingly granted, after the plea had been made that it would remove these objectionable intruders from the main library!"[1]

[1] Ruth S. Grannis in *The Book in America*, 1939 edition, p. 378.

Today, the library's services to children and teenagers are generally accepted as among its most important social functions and as an important division of its allover program. The specially furnished, separate children's room, or at least library corners reserved for children, rich and varied collections of picture books and children's story books, the presence of specially trained children's librarians, story-telling hours, exhibitions at Christmas time or in connection with other holidays and special occasions, the frequent publication of lists of recommended readings, lending services for books that may be taken home as well as permanent reference collections of books designed to answer the many and varied questions children may wish to have answered, close cooperation with the schools of a given community—all these things have come to be accepted parts of the public library's activities.

Library work with teenagers (or young adolescents) has developed somewhat more recently.

"Librarians discovered that too many of the children suddenly disappeared from libraries when they entered their teens. They were eager to enter the world of adult books, but they were bewildered and lost as readers when thrown into adult book collections without the guidance of specially trained librarians. It was obvious that they too—these young people—needed special library services. . . . Throughout the country, forward-looking citizens, alert to the needs of youth, are planning improved services appropriate to this group which must soon assume leadership in community affairs. . . . Emphasis is placed on the necessity of organizing young people's work as an adult division with two clearly defined aspects: the service to the young people themselves, involving their introduction to every kind of printed material, and the coordination of this service with city-wide, youth-serving agencies . . ."[1]

The people by and large have come to accept the public library as a kind of institutional friend, something or someone to turn to on all sorts of occasions. They have come to take for granted this ever-willing and ever-ready friend—a very good thing probably, even if their reliance on this friend sometimes takes unexpected forms. Some of the questions asked at the reference desk of any large library (and probably of many small ones as well) would surprise you. "How many bones in the human body?" "How many words in the English language?" "Have cows upper teeth?" "Can mice throw up?" "What is the gestation period of elephants?" "What are the names of Santa Claus' reindeer?" A harassed caterer called up at 3 P.M. to ask where he could buy a thousand squabs for a 7 o'clock banquet! A manufacturer of baby carriages asked where he could get a list of pregnant women living in his community!

The public library in America today is indeed a very different place from that first library in seventeenth-century Boston which was a "library and gallery for divines and scholars to meet in." One of the most important changes that have taken place is in the kinds of

[1] Quoted from *The Public Library, Plans for the Teen Age*, published by the American Library Association in 1948.

materials that a library collects and uses today. In the old days books were about the only kind of reading matter a library would carry, with the possible addition of a few journals. Today, a large variety of periodicals play a very significant role in the library, especially in science and technology, where rapid developments call for quick ways of disseminating up-to-date information. There were print rooms here and there in the old libraries. Today, the print rooms are still important, but they have changed into or have been supplemented by the picture collections, where photographs and various kinds of photographic reproductions are used in great quantities to serve many different purposes. Color reproductions of works of art have made a place for themselves alongside the books and periodicals in the library's art department, and, like the books in the circulating department, they are lent out freely to the library's patrons in more than one library today. The same thing is true of phonograph records, which are found alongside the books, and the sheet music in the library's music department.

Nor is the reading of printed materials the only kind of activity that brings people into the library today. Listening to music and story-telling, participating in discussion groups, attending a lecture or seeing a motion picture or a special exhibit—such activities are very much a part of the program of a modern public library.

The question may well be asked whether the replacement of the book by other materials and the replacement of reading by other activities in the library do not reflect an important change in the role of the book in our lives. Perhaps we are already well on the road to a kind of society which no longer needs books, a condition which Thomas Wolfe (in *The Hills Beyond*) has written of as follows:

> "It may be that some later period in the human history will dispense with the whole necessity of print, and that book-reading, book-writing, book-publishing, all the ramified accessories that have accumulated since old Gutenberg, will (through some system of psychophones, printoscopes, emphatic waves, or type telepathies; or what more of the strange and unbelievable we cannot wot of) be as prehistoric as the dinosaur."

It is to this question that I should like to devote the final chapter of this little book about books.

Conclusion

SOME THOUGHTS ON THE BOOK IN AMERICA

There are many indications that the position of the book in American life today is seriously threatened. Many other forms of entertainment and new channels of information are making strong bids for the attention of every man, woman, and child. Television and radio, the movies, the comics, and all sorts of non-bookish reading matter make their demands on the time and energy of the public. Many thoughtful people view the situation with a good deal of apprehension, while others are inclined to accept it rather calmly. What does it matter, they say, if the kind of entertainment and information which the book used to provide reaches you in various other ways, as long as it reaches you?

Those who still believe in the book know that it has some unique qualities which are very important today. Many men and women in this country are united in their belief in the good book. William Sloane, the publisher, says it in these words:[1]

"The books which a nation publishes and reads are a major part of that nation's mind, and the most basic medium of communication between peoples. It is essential that as many books as possible shall be good and useful books by this criterion."

Charles F. Bound, the banker, speaks as follows:[1]

"The book is unquestionably the most important medium of communication. In these days of crisis when the very foundations of democracy are threatened, the book publishers have a heavy responsibility to provide the basic food to strengthen our minds and hearts and provide nourishment to those seeking truth and knowledge. If they cannot keep their ships afloat in the rough economic storms ahead their ideals and their author's ideas will go down together."

Helen Haines, friend of readers and libraries, writes thus in her *Living with Books*:[1]

"Magazines are far more widely read than books; but not by those who know the joys and values of reading. Magazines and newspapers—both dominant factors in American mass culture—are no more than accessories or deterrents to reading; they do not signify that wide ranging and rich adventure in the world of books that is real reading. Magazines have their place, their own usefulness; but no magazine can take the place of standard books. There are periodicals of literary value, of scholarly, technical, or specialized importance, essential to scholars and scientific and technical workers and to men and women in every field. But if more Americans would read good books and cease reading promiscuous popular magazines, we should have a higher level of general education and intelligence."

[1] As quoted in *The Book in America*, 2nd edition, pp. 417-418.

It is obvious that if the book were seriously to lose ground or disappear altogether, something very important and precious would pass out of our lives. For this reason it is desirable that we try to find out if this is really happening, if the book is losing out or holding its own.

Many professional groups, educators, librarians, publishers, and booksellers are trying to find the answer to this question. Various kinds of studies and surveys have been made and statistics gathered. The evidence has not been altogether conclusive: there have been some contradictions and varying evidence which make it difficult to formulate a clear answer from the results of such studies. Personally I find it difficult to work with statistics. However, there are some observations which I think may throw some light on the question. Naturally, as one man's opinion, their value is somewhat limited. But the experiences of a person who has lived the first half of his life in Europe and the second in the United States, and who has spent over thirty years living with books may be of some interest.

A little more than a quarter of a century ago, when I came to the United States to live, and began to explore the world of books, I found myself frequently misled by captions in the newspapers which read something like this: "Publishers' Convention to Open on Monday," or "Society of Illustrators Holds Its Spring Show." I expected news of book publishers and book illustrators, but what I found, of course, were stories about newspaper publishers and magazine illustrators. In Europe a "publisher" was always a book publisher. You had to say "newspaper publisher" if that was what you meant.

When I went to visit some of my new friends in their houses in the suburbs, I noticed that everybody on the train was buried in his favorite newspaper or magazine, and at the house there were many magazines in the living room, and everybody could help himself. There were some books, too, on the living room shelf. But I saw that very few people had a room set aside as a library or study, with the walls lined with books, and the doors closed, such as those I had known. I met authors and literary agents and was surprised to learn that writing short stories and magazine articles was usually far more profitable than writing books.

The book publishers, too, seemed very interested in newspapers. They were eager to reprint in periodicals the books which they bought from their authors. Books to be reprinted in a periodical? In Europe, it had always been the other way round. And why did the publishers think that newspaper publicity for their books was so important? At home I had learned that it did not pay to advertise a book in a daily paper. It was the bookseller's job to sell the book to the public. All you could do as a publisher was to sell your book to the bookstores. But here, in America, I learned with amazement that there were many cities, large and small, which had to get along without a regular bookstore, without a place exclusively or even primarily devoted to the selling of books, and, incidentally, a social center for all people with literary and bookish interests. In this fact I recognized one of the reasons why public library service in this country has come to play such an important part in many communities and why it has developed so amazingly in the last hundred years. I had heard about that, but nobody had explained that the public library was really doing many of the things in the American community which in Europe the local bookstore was doing.

The conclusion was inescapable. Obviously, in America, the newspaper and the magazine were more important, from almost every point of view, than the book. Of course it would be absurd to say that the periodical press in Europe was not of immense importance too. But the world of the book had its own independent traditions there, which were older and more substantial than the world of periodicals. Here, the book seemed to live in a sort of dependence—not quite on its own, a somewhat underprivileged younger brother of the powerful periodical press.

It was only natural that I should try to find the reasons for these differences. Gradually, I discovered the truth. It was something that no one on either side of the Atlantic had told me about, and nothing was written about it in the many books, articles, and pamphlets on American books and printing which I began to consult.

Do you know the old saying that "a stone placed at the source of a river may alter its entire course"? Perhaps this is not literally true, but it is a good way of saying that if something very important happens at a very early stage, it may have tremendous consequences. We know this is true in human lives. Important experiences in early childhood can have a profound effect on a person's life.

The reason why the role of books and printing on one side of the Atlantic Ocean is different from that on the other can be found at the very source of the history of printing in America.

One need only consider under what different conditions and for what different purposes printing was introduced and was spread in the old world and the new. In Europe, printing was started in settled communities that were centuries old. It was a new, mechanical way of providing more and cheaper copies of all sorts of texts which, as manuscripts, were already well-established parts of the cultural tradition of the old world. In America, printing almost immediately became an important factor of colonization and soon an instrument of active westward expansion of the nation. The European press primarily nourished thought; the American, action. In Europe printing from the beginning meant "books"; in America almost from the start, "newspapers." In Europe the newspaper press was an offspring of the long-established book press, while in America, by contrast, it was introduced into a vacuum and became the dominant form of printing. Occasionally, the busy pioneer printer would produce a book, along with newspapers, pamphlets, commercial announcements, bills, and legal forms. But when he did so, it was a time-consuming project, usually conducted at odd moments during slack periods and without sufficient equipment.

Nothing could be more significant for the recognition of the superior role of the periodical press in the young American democracy than a letter written by George Washington to Mathew Carey on June 25, 1788: "I consider such easy vehicles of knowledge as more highly calculated than any other to preserve the liberty, stimulate the industry and meliorate the morals of an enlightened and free people." Almost a century later, Dr. Holland, editor of *Scribner's Monthly*, wrote this of the magazine in 1873: "It stands in the very front rank of the agents of civilization."

In the nineteenth century, to an even greater extent than before, the history of printing in America, in terms of first presses established in new communities, territories, and states, became identified with the history of American journalism. The adventurous migration of the press, its transportation by wagon, boat, pack horse, and mule—over the mountains, across the plains, and along the almost virgin rivers—was first and foremost for the printing of newspapers. The fight for the freedom of the press in America arose solely over matter published in newspapers.

It was mainly for magazine writing that a class of professional men of letters developed in America. Authorship during the years of the young republic was greatly influenced by this fact. Novels, on the whole,

The pioneer press on a covered wagon

were not profitable enough to engage the full time of most writers, and so, understandably enough, they wrote the short story or essay for the better paying periodicals. To this circumstance we owe the galvanic development of the characteristic American short story, which in turn helped the sharp rise in the popularity of the periodical.

The industrialization of printing, the conversion of a craft into an instrument of mass production, was an international development, but in America it received its most powerful impetus from the demands of the periodical press.

Labor organization in the printing industry started early in America and its role is considered epochmaking in the general history of the union movement. Again, it was the fundamental political, social, and economic importance of the periodical press which placed such a powerful weapon into the hands of the men who were directly responsible for the functioning of this vital, complicated mechanism.

To sum this all up, there is no question that the traditional superiority of the periodical over the book constitutes one of the chief and most characteristic points of difference between American and European culture. But what does that teach us about the position of the book in America today and about its future? The most important lesson, it seems to me, is this: If we think of the competition of other media of communication as an especially dangerous threat to the book, then we must realize that the book in America has always had to live in the face of that kind of competition. Since the beginning of printing in the English-speaking colonies of North America, the book has survived three hundred years of struggle for a place in the sun, and it has come through in a very creditable manner. Compared with the three hundred years of competition with the periodical press, the struggle with all the other media combined is a very recent development, not older than twenty-five or fifty years at most. There is distinct comfort in the thought that the book is a seasoned veteran in this battle.

There is also the thought that the new media so far have not shown themselves particularly well suited to taking over some of the most important functions of the book in our lives. It is a very curious fact that in their initial phases the great new inventions in communication have not served great new ideas. Contrary to many people's expectations, the most advanced technological devices have not been the mouthpiece of advanced thinking or progressive artistic creation. The reason for this is not difficult to see. The new media are mass media, and economic pressure makes it necessary for them to appeal to the taste of the masses, at least during the early stages of development. By comparison, the book, a mature and seasoned medium with highly developed production methods and long-established channels of distribution to many different groups of readers, is generally in a far better position to serve new thought and new artistic expression.

In spite of media competition and of many economic difficulties, the American book in the last quarter of a century has seen encouraging advance in several important ways. The publishing trade at large is in a far better position than ever before to serve the varying tastes of different groups. There has been a noticeable increase in certain kinds of special publishing, particularly in the fields of art and in psychology and psychiatry, but in various other fields as well. Also, the rapid increase in the number of university presses (already discussed on page 39), scattered throughout the country rather than concentrated in New York, marks a most valuable advance in providing many special kinds of books for many groups of specialized interest.

Also in the last quarter of a century, there has been a steadily growing appreciation of old and rare books, a taste formerly reserved for the wealthy private collector. Whereas twenty-five years ago the number of curators of rare books serving in American university and public libraries could be counted on the fingers of one hand, a person's both hands and toes would not be sufficient to count them today.

Fine printing and good book design, twenty-five years ago, were reserved for private press books and limited editions. As a result of a truly great renaissance of the graphic arts in America, not only many trade books, but also a large number of textbooks and schoolbooks, juveniles, children's picture books, and quite a few other special kinds of books have now become things of beauty.

Last but not least, we must remember that the comparatively recent arrival on the literary scene of the paper-back book is causing what many people think of as one of the greatest revolutions in reading ever to have occurred.

All these developments of the last quarter of a century, seen together, are really very encouraging. There is good reason to hope that the book will not only hold its own but contribute in its particular way to the enrichment of our lives in the years ahead.

I would like to conclude this little book about books with a few words which might be called

A MID-TWENTIETH-CENTURY BOOKMAN'S CREDO

The Book:

The single voice of the individual creator speaking clearly, in words, in images, through the message of its contents as well as through the language of form, to the individual reader, who lives in a world which makes it all too easy to let others tell you what you should like, what you should think, how you should act—what kind of a person you should be.

The book is among the most powerful weapons in the hands of the individual who still takes time to think where he or she is, where he is going, what sort of a person he wants to be, and how he can help others find out what kind of persons they want to be.

SUGGESTED BOOKS FOR FURTHER READING

BENNETT, PAUL A. (EDIT.) *Books and Printing: A Treasury for Typophiles*. Cleveland & New York, World, 1951.
A colorful and lively anthology of essays on matters typographic, on books, their printing, and some of the fascinating steps along the way. The list of contributors reads like a "Who's Who" in twentieth-century graphic arts.

CERAM, C. W. *Gods, Graves and Scholars: The Story of Archaeology*. New York, Knopf, 1952.
This is a general book about archaeology, but the parts about Egypt and Mesopotamia contain interesting information on early inscriptions, how they were dug up and deciphered.

CHIERA, EDWARD. *They Wrote on Clay: The Babylonian Tablets Speak Today*. Chicago, University of Chicago Press, 1938.
This book offers an opportunity to get close to these amazing ancestors of our books and to understand them as fully as anybody could wish to understand them without actually studying the language and the script.

CLEETON, GLEN U. & PITKIN, CHARLES W. *General Printing*. Bloomington, Ill., McKnight & McKnight, 1941.
A practical textbook for printing students, with excellent photographic illustrations of the various operations.

Cockerell, Douglas. *Bookbinding and the Care of Books: A Handbook for Bookbinders and Librarians.* London, Pitman, 1948 (4th edition).
Although somewhat outmoded in the kinds of decoration recommended, this is still one of the most valuable explanations of the technique of hand binding as it is practiced today.

Groesbeck, Harry A. *Processes of Reproduction.* "The Dolphin," No. 1. New York, Limited Editions Club, 1933.
A simple and sound explanation of pictorial reproduction through the various photomechanical processes.

Hogben, Lancelot. *From Cave Painting to Comic Strip.* New York, Chanticleer Press, 1949.
A brilliant book, full of fascinating and stimulating ideas. Not an easy book to read, but the many illustrations and diagrams are a great help.

Hunter, Dard. *The History and Technique of an Ancient Craft.* New York, Knopf, 1947 (2nd edition).
The best and most complete book on paper making in the English language.

Ilin, M. (Beatrice Kincead, transl.). *Black on White: The Story of Books.* Philadelphia, Lippincott, 1932.
In simple and entertaining words Ilin tells the story of the book, its ancestors, its early forms, and the changes to our modern formats—a book which reads like a fairy tale.

Karch, R. Randolph. *Graphic Arts Procedures.* Chicago, American Technical Society, 1948.
A good general introduction to practical printing, written especially for students learning about graphic arts in the schools, and for apprentices in the printing trades.

Lehmann-Haupt, Hellmut. *One Hundred Books about Bookmaking: A Guide to the Study and Appreciation of Printing.* New York, Columbia, 1949.
This is not a complete bibliography of printing and bookmak-

ing, but a selected reading list, in nine sections, of good books of permanent value.

——*The Terrible Gustave Doré.* New York, 1943
——*Peter Schoeffer of Gernsheim and Mainz.* Rochester, 1950.
——(in collaboration with HANNAH D. FRENCH and JOSEPH W. ROGERS) *Bookbinding in America.* Portland, Maine, 1941.

LEHMANN-HAUPT, HELLMUT (EDIT.) in collaboration with LAWRENCE C. WROTH and ROLLO G. SILVER. *The Book in America: A History of the Making and Selling of Books in the United States.* New York, Bowker, 1951 (2nd edition).
A general, straightforward survey of printing and the allied crafts and of publishing and bookselling, from colonial beginnings to the present.

MCMURTRIE, DOUGLAS C. *The Story of Printing & Bookmaking.* (3rd edition revised under present title.) New York, Oxford, 1943.
In spite of certain weaknesses, this is the most successful history of printing hitherto attempted by a single author.

MORISON, STANLEY. *First Principles of Typography.* New York, Macmillan, 1936.
A simple and clear statement on the use of type.

MUELLER, HANS ALEXANDER. *How I Make Woodcuts and Wood Engravings.* New York, American Artists Group, 1945.
An excellent guide, by one of the masters of the craft.

MYRICK, FRANK B. *A Primer in Book Production.* New York, Bookbinding & Book Production, 1946 (2nd printing).
A useful survey of book manufacturing, from the estimating of copy to the finished volume.

OGG, OSCAR. *The 26 Letters.* New York, Crowell, 1948.
The story of the 26 letters of our alphabet, from pre-historic beginnings to the machine age. Beautifully illustrated with pictures and hand lettering by the author.

THOMAS, DAVID. *Type for Print, or What the Beginner Should Know about Typefounding, Letter-Design, and Type Faces.* London, Whitaker, 1947 (2nd edition).
A good introduction to the world of type faces.

THOMPSON, TOMMY. *The ABC of Our Alphabet.* London & New York, Studio, 1945 (2nd edition).
A fresh approach and direct language characterize this book which tells the development of our alphabet. It is illustrated throughout with uncomplicated eloquent diagrams.

TSCHICHOLD, JAN. *Designing Books.* New York, Wittenborn, Schultz, Inc.
Probably the best explanation in book form on how to design a book.

Acknowledgments

Until a short time before going to press, this book had no satisfactory title. I discussed this difficulty with my family and, a week later, my youngest son, then aged six, came up with the title, *The Life of the Book*. His older brothers, aged thirteen, seventeen, and twenty-one, have also been helpful. From time to time, they have allowed me to read to them and to some of their friends portions from the manuscript, and have assisted me in deciding what would and would not interest other people of their age levels.

As on many previous occasions, the New York Public Library has been helpful in numerous ways. I am especially appreciative of the assistance received from Miss Margaret C. Scoggin and Miss Esther Walls of the Office of Young Peoples' Services, from Miss Mary E. Neubert, coordinator of Book Ordering, and from Mr. Gerritt Fielstra of the Reference Division.

Permission to reprint or otherwise make use of material in their publications was generously granted by the R. R. Bowker Company, the Columbia University Press, Crown Publishers, The Macmillan Company, H. P. Kraus, and George McKibbin & Sons, all in New York City.

Mr. Stephens Mitchell in Atlanta, Georgia, representing the Margaret Mitchell Marsh Estate, responded most kindly to my request for information about the writing and publishing of *Gone with the Wind*.

Assistance in selecting illustrations and permission to reproduce pictorial material in this book was generously granted by the following individuals, institutions and firms: The late William A. Dwiggins in Hingham, Mass., the Morgan Library, and the School of Library Service, Columbia University, both in New York City; the Mergenthaler Linotype Company in Brooklyn, N. Y.; the Lanston Monotype Machine Company in Philadelphia; the rare book firm of H. P. Kraus in New York City. The examples of medieval writing (p. 62) were reproduced from *The Roman Letter*, published by R. R. Donnelley & Sons in Chicago (which lists the original sources of the reproductions used).

Valuable advice was given me by Miss Laura E. Vroman, High School Librarian at Great Neck, N. Y., Mr. John Cook Wyllie, Librarian of the University of Virginia, and Mr. Ferdy J. Tagle, Principal of the New York School of Printing.

Of the many fellow members in the book trade who on various occasions have helped answer questions and furnish valuable information, I would like to mention especially Milton Glick, George T. Goodspeed, Chandler Graniss, Arthur Hale, John S. Kebebian, Sol M. Malkin, and Murray Salomon.

I am most grateful to my wife for having patiently deciphered what I am told is illegible handwriting when turning the manuscript of this book into a typescript fit to be sent to the printer.

H.L.-H.

Index